Plant Cells
and Tissues

The Green World

Plant Cells and Tissues

Nicholas Stephens

Series Editor
William G. Hopkins
Professor Emeritus of Biology
University of Western Ontario

CHELSEA HOUSE
PUBLISHERS
An imprint of Infobase Publishing

Plant Cells and Tissues

Copyright © 2006 by Infobase Publishing

All rights reserved. No part of this book may be reproduced or utilized in any form or by any means, electronic or mechanical, including photocopying, recording, or by any information storage or retrieval systems, without permission in writing from the publisher. For information contact:

Chelsea House
An imprint of Infobase Publishing
132 West 31st Street
New York NY 10001

Library of Congress Cataloging-in-Publication Data

Stephens, Nicholas
 Plant cells and tissues / Nicholas Stephens.
    p. cm. — (The green world)
 ISBN 0-7910-8560-0
 1. Plants cells and tissues—Juvenile literature. I. Title. II. Green world. (Philadelphia, Pa.)
 QK725.S782 2006
 571.6'2—dc22   2005032186

Chelsea House books are available at special discounts when purchased in bulk quantities for businesses, associations, institutions, or sales promotions. Please call our Special Sales Department in New York at (212) 967-8800 or (800) 322-8755.

You can find Chelsea House on the World Wide Web at http://www.chelseahouse.com

Text and cover design by Keith Trego

Printed in the United States of America

Bang 21C 10 9 8 7 6 5 4 3 2 1

This book is printed on acid-free paper.

All links, web addresses, and Internet search terms were checked and verified to be correct at the time of publication. Because of the dynamic nature of the web, some addresses and links may have changed since publication and may no longer be valid.

Table of Contents

Introduction

By William G. Hopkins

"Have you thanked a green plant today?" reads a popular bumper sticker. Indeed, we should thank green plants for providing the food we eat, fiber for the clothing we wear, wood for building our houses, and the oxygen we breathe. Without plants, humans and other animals simply could not exist. Psychologists tell us that plants also provide a sense of well-being and peace of mind, which is why we preserve forested parks in our cities, surround our homes with gardens, and install plants and flowers in our homes and workplaces. Gifts of flowers are the most popular way to acknowledge weddings, funerals, and other events of passage. Gardening is one of the fastest growing hobbies in North America and the production of ornamental plants contributes billions of dollars annually to the economy.

Human history has been strongly influenced by plants. The rise of agriculture in the Fertile Crescent of Mesopotamia brought previously scattered hunter-gatherers together into villages. Ever since, the availability of land and water for cultivating plants has been a major factor in determining the location of human settlements. World exploration and discovery was driven by the search for herbs and spices. The cultivation of New World crops—sugar, cotton, and tobacco—was responsible for the introduction of slavery to America, the human and social consequences of which are still with us. The push westward by English colonists into the rich lands of the Ohio River Valley in the mid-1700s was driven by the need to increase corn production and was a factor in precipitating the French and Indian War. The Irish Potato Famine in 1847 set in motion a wave of migration, mostly to North America, that would reduce the population of Ireland by half over the next 50 years.

As a young university instructor directing biology tutorials in a classroom that looked out over a wooded area, I would ask each group of students to look out the window and tell me what they saw. More often than not, the question would be met with a blank, questioning look. Plants are so much a part of our environment and the fabric of our everyday lives that they rarely register in our conscious thought. Yet today, faced with disappearing rainforests, exploding population growth, urban sprawl, and concerns about climate change, the productive capacity of global agricultural and forestry ecosystems is put under increasing pressure. Understanding plants is even more essential as we attempt to build a sustainable environment for the future.

THE GREEN WORLD series opens doors to the world of plants. The series describes what plants are, what plants do, and where plants fit into the overall circle of life. *Plant Cells and Tissues* explores the microscopic units that all plants are composed of: cells. It describes how millions of cells work together as tissues to move materials throughout the plant body, gather water and minerals from the soil, and convert carbon dioxide into sugar using energy from the sun.

William G. Hopkins
Professor Emeritus of Biology
University of Western Ontario

There is a way that nature speaks, that land speaks.
Most of the time, we are simply not patient enough,
quiet enough, to pay attention to the story.

— Linda Hogan

Portrait of a Plant

Plants are among the most amazing organisms on Earth. They are record-breakers: the most massive individual life-form, a giant sequoia, weighs 2,000 tons (roughly equal to 15 blue whales). The oldest single living thing alive today, California's bristlecone pine tree, is estimated to be nearly 5,000 years old (making it a seedling around the time that the Sumerians invented writing). They are necessities for humans: plants feed us, clothe us, and shelter us. Plants give us oxygen to breathe, fuel to burn for warmth, and medicine to keep us healthy. They are diverse and unique: Venus flytraps, which grow in nutrient-poor bogs, have fast-closing leaves that ensnare and digest insects for food; the corpse flower, whose bloom measures as high as 9 feet, mimics the smell of a rotting animal corpse to trick beetles into pollinating it. Plants are almost everywhere we look, from moss in Antarctica to tropical rainforests, painting the land green when viewed from space and making our world nothing short of fantastic.

BOTANY: THE STUDY OF PLANTS

People have been studying plants for thousands of years, a discipline called botany. Biologically, plants are an extraordinary group of organisms. They grow to enormous sizes and reproduce in great numbers using the simplest ingredients: water from the ground, carbon dioxide from the air, energy from the sun, and minerals from the soil. Economically, plants are important sources of revenue. Many foods, medicines, and materials come from plants, which explains why millions of dollars are spent every year on researching them. Plants are also ecologically important: photosynthesis initially produces most of the food in an ecosystem.

Plants are so strikingly diverse, ranging from liverworts to tulips, that it is difficult to provide an all-encompassing definition without unjustly generalizing. It is tempting to say that all plants perform **photosynthesis**, the process by which the plant uses the

4

sun's energy to convert carbon dioxide into sugar for food. There are, however, several examples of nonphotosynthetic, parasitic plants that steal food from other plants like a thief who siphons gasoline from another's automobile. To say that all plants grow in the soil would neglect the hydrophytes that grow in water, such as duckweed, or the epiphytes, such as orchids, that grow on trees (Figure 1.1).

The one defining characteristic that all plants share with one another is their ancestry. A person's extended family (cousins, aunts, uncles, grandparents) may be very similar to one another, or as different as night and day, but they are all related to each other. Just as you and your cousins share common ancestry (your grandparents), so too are plants and green algae connected by a common ancestor that lived millions of years ago. In this respect, plants may be thought of as relatives to green algae, whose ancestors colonized the land. The task of botanists, then, is to describe and study this diverse group of organisms.

Plants belong to a group of organisms called **eukaryotes**. Eukaryotes are structurally complex organisms, which means that several functions take place within organelles of the cell, particularly the **nucleus** (the "brain" of a cell), and by the **cytoskeleton**. Eukaryotes include all animals, fungi, algae, and protists. This major group of species is distinct from the **prokaryotes** of the planet, which include bacteria and **archaea** (microorganisms that live in extreme environments). Prokaryotes are surrounded by a membrane and cell wall, and they lack organelles. Eukaryotes are typically much larger and much more complex than prokaryotes. The major features of a eukaryotic cell are discussed in Chapter 2.

Seed Plants: Familiar Faces of the Green World

Seed plants are usually more familiar and more relevant to a person's daily life than, for instance, ferns or hornworts because they are used for food and materials. Seed plants, as their name

Figure 1.1 Plants are one of the most diverse organisms on Earth. They can grow almost anywhere, from soil to ocean water. Epiphytes, such as the orchids shown here, grow on trees.

implies, produce **seeds**: tiny, protected units with dormant, baby plants inside of them. Seeds can disperse great distances and can survive for a long period of time: seeds of arctic lupine (*Lupinus arcticus*) found in Alaska were germinated after an estimated dormancy of 10,000 years![1]

The first seed plants appear in the fossil record around 365 million years ago. Today, there are two classes of living seed plants: **gymnosperms** and **angiosperms**. Gymnosperms, whose name means "naked seed," have been around much longer than angiosperms (flowering plants). Examples of today's gymnosperms include conifers such as pine trees, and *Ginkgo biloba*, which is a tree planted in many urban areas.

Angiosperms are the flowering plants of Earth. The oldest fossil of an angiosperm is only about 135 million years old. It is estimated that there are about 235,000 flowering species in the world today, an impressive number for such a relatively new group of organisms. Roughly speaking, there are two major types of angiosperms: **monocotyledons** (monocots) and **dicotyledons** (eudicots). Monocots such as corn (*Zea mays*) and orchids typically have only one **cotyledon** (seed leaf) and have floral parts (e.g., petals) in multiples of three. True dicots, such as cucumbers (*Cucumis sativus*), sunflowers (*Helianthus annuus*), and peas (*Pisum sativum*), usually have two cotyledons and floral parts in multiples of four or five.

CELLS: THE UNITS OF LIFE

Biologists have a hard time agreeing on a definition of "life," though they generally agree that the basic unit of all living organisms is the **cell** (Figure 1.2). A cell has all of the necessary features that are required for life, enabling many organisms, such as prokaryotes, to exist as single cells. Complex organisms, such as plants and animals, are also composed of many cells, though they each begin their lives as a single cell. **Viruses** are excluded from this working definition of life because they require a host cell to replicate; without cells, viruses would cease to exist.

What Are Cells?

The concept of a cell is relatively new to biology. Robert Hooke first coined the term "cell" in 1665, following his observation of

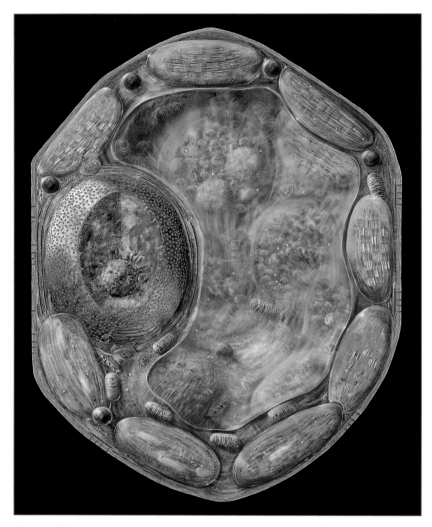

Figure 1.2 A cell has all of the necessary features that are required for life. Complex organisms, such as plants and animals, are composed of many cells. Plant cell structure includes the cell wall (yellow), chloroplasts (green ovals circling the cell), the nucleus (pink, center left), and mitochondria (small orange/yellow ovals).

a slice of cork through a homemade microscope. The microscopic chambers that he saw did not gain their deserved appreciation until the mid-1800s, when botanists and zoologists realized that cells were the fundamental building blocks of all plants and animals. Today, we recognize that cells are the sites of an organism's chemical reactions, including conversion of food into energy and production of new molecules or structures. A cell is able to accumulate materials and perform such processes because it isolates its interior from its external environment.

Cells are usually quite small, often too small to be seen without a microscope. It is for this reason that the presence and importance of the cell were unknown until only recently. A cell cannot have a very large volume because it is limited by the biochemical requirement of a large surface area. Cells need extensive contact with their surroundings so that they may acquire enough food or other molecules necessary for life. A large surface area, relative to the cell volume, is also important because it allows the cell to get rid of waste products and toxic compounds. Single-celled organisms, such as bacteria, respond to this surface area constraint by remaining microscopically small. Large organisms, such as plants, are able to maintain an adequate surface area by composing their bodies of many individual cells: this achieves a large volume while also providing each cell with an appropriate surface area for materials exchange.

Where Do Cells Come From?

No cell has ever been observed to be created from its raw components; instead, cells are produced by preexisting cells alone. This observation that cells only arise from other cells (discussed in Chapter 4) has led to the theory that all modern cells can be traced back to a single, primitive cell that existed at least 3.5 billion years ago. According to this theory, each cell on the planet is the distant descendent of a single progenitor in the same way that every cell in your body is derived from the products of a single precursor. The theory, however, seems to present a chicken-and-egg paradox: if cells only come from other cells, then from where did the first one arise? No one knows where, when, or how the first cell appeared on Earth, but its descendants are abundant today throughout the planet.

LEVELS OF ORGANIZATION: CELLS, TISSUES, AND ORGANS

Botanists study plants at many different levels, from cells to trees to forests. Each successively higher level of complexity brings with it the advantage of each of its components working together. Chapters 5–8 focus on the two organizational levels above cells: tissues and organs.

A Word About Scale

Just how small is *small*? Well, it all depends on scale. To a 6-foot-tall (1.82 meter) person, a millimeter (mm) is a tiny distance; to a microscopic bacterium such as *Escherichia coli*, a millimeter is 2,000 times longer than its entire length.

Scientists frequently use the metric system because it is easy to compare small and large quantities. In this system, 1 meter (3.28 feet), for example, equals 100 centimeters (cm); likewise, 1 centimeter equals 0.01 meters. Even smaller units of length are the micrometer (μm) and nanometer (nm). A micrometer is one million times shorter than a meter and a nanometer is one billion times shorter than a meter!

To offer an appreciation of just how small a micrometer or nanometer is, consider the paper on which this text is printed. Standard sheets of paper are one-tenth of a millimeter in thickness, or 0.1 mm. By converting millimeters to micrometers and nanometers, this paper is estimated to be 100 micrometers or 100,000 nanometers thick. Stated another way, one nanometer is approximately 100,000 times smaller than the thickness of this page.

Making conversions such as this can be useful when reading a scientific book or article. It helps to make a foreign unit of measurement like a nanometer bear meaning with respect to your own experiences.

A collection of cells that have common structures and function is called a **tissue**. Animals have four categories of tissues—epithelial, nervous, connective, and muscular—each of which has a specific function. These tissues are sufficient for an animal, whose survival generally involves moving around. A plant, however, spends its life in a fixed position and, therefore, has evolved a very different set of tissues that are better suited for a photosynthetic, immobile life. The tissues of a typical seed plant, as well as the cell types found in them, are discussed in detail in Chapter 5.

An **organ** is a structure that is composed of multiple tissues. Animals have numerous organs. Each of these organs has a special function that contributes to an animalistic way of life: a brain for reasoning, a heart for pumping blood, lungs for breathing, and so on. The bodies of plants, like animals, combine their tissues into organs that perform specific functions. The organs of plants—roots, stems, and leaves—have been optimized for a vegetative lifestyle. Chapters 6, 7, and 8 describe each of these organs in detail.

In order to appreciate the diversity of plant form and function, we must first start with the smallest component, the cell. Chapter 2 will introduce the plant cell in greater detail, focusing on the shared features of all eukaryotes.

2 Introduction to the Plant Cell

The uniformity of earth's life, more astonishing than its diversity, is accountable by the high probability that we derived, originally, from some single cell, fertilized in a bolt of lightning as the earth cooled.

— Lewis Thomas

Introduction to the Plant Cell

What could starfish, pine trees, bald eagles, and raspberries possibly have in common with each other? Indeed, the dramatic differences between plants and animals sometimes make it difficult to appreciate the similarities between the two groups. Actually, all eukaryotes share certain characteristics that make them similar, most notably on a cellular level.

THE PLASMA MEMBRANE

The **plasma membrane** is a thin sheath that surrounds the cellular contents of all living cells, eukaryotic and prokaryotic. It separates the interior of each cell from the outside world like an international border separates two countries: some items are allowed to cross while others are not. This characteristic of selective passage makes the plasma membrane a **semipermeable** barrier. Water is one material that may cross the membrane freely.

On a chemical level, the plasma membrane consists of **proteins** (molecular machines) floating around in a flexible sea of **lipids**, which make up fats and oils. The lipid molecules of membranes consist of a **hydrophilic** (water-loving) head and long, **hydrophobic** (water-fearing) tails. The inside and outside of cells consist mostly of water, and, as a consequence, the lipid molecules orient themselves so that their tails come together and their heads face the water. As a result, a double sheet known as a **lipid bilayer** surrounds cells (Figure 2.1).

Embedded within this lipid bilayer and attached to its surfaces are membrane proteins that provide countless services for the cell. Many proteins form passageways for molecules to enter and exit the cell; some of these passageways are always open, some may be opened and closed, while others use energy to actively pump molecules across the plasma membrane as a means of doing work. A large number of membrane proteins act as receptors for specific chemicals such as hormones or wound signals, which help a cell respond to a changing environment. Proteins are essential components of the plasma membrane, as

14

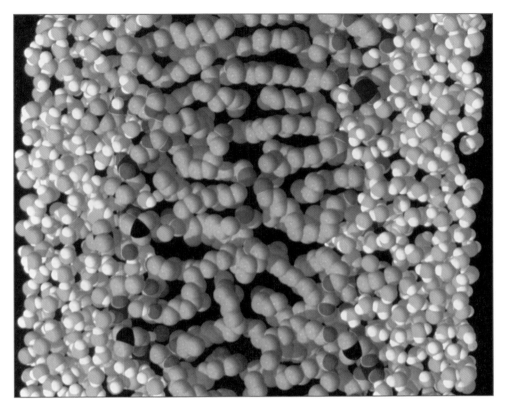

Figure 2.1 Phospholipid bilayers form the membranes around all living cells. The cell membrane is made of hydrophilic (water-loving) heads and hydrophobic (water-fearing) tails. The hydrophobic part of the phospholipid is a fatty acid chain, shown here in blue. The molecules line up in two sheets, with the fatty acid chains forming a hydrophobic layer in the middle. The hydrophilic surfaces of the membrane are shown here in yellow and white.

they connect the interior of the cell with its neighboring cells and its environment.

As a cell grows in size, it must increase the amount of surrounding membrane to keep from exploding. Additional membrane is added into the cell surface by fusing **membrane-bound vesicles** to the inner surface of the plasma membrane. Vesicles are small spheres of lipid bilayer within the cell that surround a liquid center. These vesicles may contain membrane proteins on their surfaces that become incorporated into the greater plasma membrane and/or materials that, upon vesicle fusion, get dumped into the cell's exterior environment; this latter process is called **secretion.**

CYTOSOL AND CYTOSKELETON:
A MATRIX OF LIQUID AND STRUCTURAL ELEMENTS

Within the plasma membrane is a soupy solution known as the **cytosol.** Cytosol is a thick mixture of salts and organic molecules dissolved in water that fills the interior of the cell. This liquid medium is important because it allows nutrients and molecular building blocks to diffuse throughout the cell to wherever they are needed. The cytosol and all of its contents, excluding the nucleus, are collectively called **cytoplasm.**

The cytoskeleton is an intricate network of filamentous proteins that runs throughout the cytosol. As the name suggests, the cytoskeleton provides a framework for a cell much the same way that bones provide a framework for human bodies. In addition to its structural role, the cytoskeleton also functions as a highway system for **molecular motors**—energy-burning proteins that move **organelles** (membrane-bound component of the cell), vesicles, and even other proteins throughout the cytosol.

Microtubules are hollow cytoskeletal tubes that are necessary for proper cellular function. A single microtubule consists of many protein subunits, called **tubulin,** stacked in a long, narrow coil that is 24 nanometers in diameter. These long structures are continuously **polymerizing** (adding new subunits) and **degrading** (losing subunits), thus they are constantly elongating and shrinking. They provide support to the cell, direct vesicle-bearing molecular motors to the plasma membrane, and are crucial players in cell division (see Chapter 4).

Microfilaments, which are smaller than microtubules (5–7 nanometers in diameter), are also important cytoskeletal elements. The filaments consist of **actin** proteins stacked in a long column and act as highways for the molecular motor **myosin** to move along. The coactions of actin and myosin (which are the proteins responsible for muscle movement in animals) serve in organelle movement and vesicle transport.

THE NUCLEUS: INFORMATION-STORAGE UNIT

The defining characteristic of a eukaryotic cell is its nucleus (plural, nuclei); even the word *eukaryotic* means "having a true nucleus." Most plant cells have only one nucleus, which can be seen under a low-power microscope. Nuclei contain all of the information for proteins, the molecular machines and structural elements that make a cell function.

The structure of the nucleus is relatively simple. It is surrounded by two lipid bilayers, which collectively are called the **nuclear envelope**. Large pores made of proteins perforate the envelopes so that they are selectively permeable. The interior of the nucleus is filled with a solution that is similar to cytosol.

Inside the nucleus are large molecules of **deoxyribonucleic acid (DNA)**. A DNA molecule is a double helix that is formed by two strands, much like a spirally twisted ladder. The rungs of this ladder are made of the paired nitrogenous bases (**base pairs**) of the two strands. There are four types of **nitrogenous bases** found in DNA: **adenine** (A), **guanine** (G), **cytosine** (C), and **thymine** (T). Due to their chemical natures, adenine always binds with thymine and guanine always binds with cytosine. The two strands of a DNA double helix are said to be **complementary** because, though they both have completely different sequences, their nitrogenous bases will bind to one another due to the rules of base pairing. The tops and bottoms of Lego blocks, or the north and south ends of a magnet, are other examples of complementary items; the opposites come together. DNA is usually bound to proteins, a combination that is known as **chromatin**. Chromatin stains easily with certain chemicals and may be seen with a light microscope.

Nondividing cells may also contain a **nucleolus** (plural, nucleoli), a visibly distinct, dense cluster of granule-like objects. The granules are **ribosomes** (protein-building machinery) that are in the process of being synthesized and assembled. A particular nucleus may contain more than one nucleolus.

DNA contains information for all of the proteins that an organism makes. The information for a particular protein is stored as a specific sequence of nitrogenous bases (A, C, G, and T) that is called a **gene**. A gene may be thousands of base pairs in length. Note that the "language" of DNA, in which genes are the "words," has a four-character "alphabet": this becomes significant when genetic instructions must be translated into the language of proteins, which has an alphabet of 20 **amino acids**.

TRANSCRIPTION AND TRANSLATION

A protein may be made of one or more **polypeptides** (chains of amino acids that are linked together). The process by which the sequence of a gene dictates the amino acid sequence of a polypeptide involves two major stages: **transcription** and **translation**.

Transcription: From DNA to RNA

In order to transmit the instructions of a gene from the nucleus to the protein-sequencing machinery located in the cytoplasm, a mobile messenger is needed to carry the information. Transcription of a particular gene occurs in the nucleus and involves copying the DNA sequence onto an **RNA** intermediate. RNA (ribonucleic acid) is structurally similar to DNA except for a few differences. The sugar component of the RNA molecule (ribose) has an additional oxygen molecule on it, unlike the sugar component of DNA (deoxyribose). RNA is usually a single-stranded molecule, whereas DNA is double stranded. Furthermore, the nitrogenous base "alphabet" of RNA has replaced thymine (T) with **uracil** (U); adenine, cytosine, and guanine are present in both DNA and RNA.

When a gene becomes activated by certain cellular conditions, then nuclear proteins produce a complimentary RNA strand. Transcribed RNA can be thought of like a photographic negative: between the original scene and the eventual photograph is an inverse image that stores the information. Once synthesized, the RNA molecule is modified (a step unique to eukaryotes) so that it can be transported out of the nucleus into the cytosol. Following modification, the RNA is called **messenger RNA** (mRNA) because it carries the message of the gene and can now be used to make a protein.

Translation: From RNA to Polypeptide

Translation of the mRNA instructions into a polypeptide sequence occurs in the cytosol on ribosomes. Ribosomes are made of two subunits, one large and one small. Each subunit is composed of both protein and RNA that were synthesized in the nucleus. Ribosomes may be either free-floating in the cytosol or bound to the **endoplasmic reticulum**. There may be millions of ribosomes in a given cell.

The code-breaking step of translation involves two different RNA molecules. The mRNA molecule, which carries the gene information from the nucleus, docks onto a ribosome in preparation for polypeptide synthesis. The molecule that deciphers the mRNA sequence into an appropriate polypeptide sequence is **transfer RNA** (**tRNA**). A tRNA molecule consists of a single, short strand of RNA (only about 80 bases) that is folded back. At one end of the tRNA molecule is a site where a specific amino acid can attach. At the opposite end of the molecule is a sequence of three bases, called the **anticodon**. Anticodons have complimentary sequences to **codons** on mRNA (also sequences of three bases). There are 64 different codons: one that signals "start," three that signal "stop," and 60 that correspond to the 20 amino acids. The translation from mRNA codons to polypeptides is possible because tRNA molecules contain a specific anticodon and a specific amino acid cargo.

Ribosomes act like molecular factories that facilitate the production of polypeptides. Within the cytosol, at any given moment, there is a pool of tRNA molecules with amino acids as cargo. mRNA is fed between the two ribosomal subunits during translation, and amino-acid-carrying tRNA molecules bind their anticodons to the appropriate codons. When two tRNAs bind to neighboring mRNA codons, the amino acids that they are carrying come in close proximity and bind to each other (they prefer to bind to one another than to stay bound to the tRNA). As the mRNA progresses through the ribosome, this process repeats over and over, building a chain of amino acids (a polypeptide). The order of amino acids, each of which has distinct physical properties, influences the structure and function of the resulting polypeptide. When a **stop codon** is reached on the mRNA strand, the polypeptide is released from the ribosome, thus completing the process of translation.

THE ENDOPLASMIC RETICULUM

An intricate network of membrane-bound compartments fills a large portion of the cytosol. This network, called the endoplasmic reticulum (ER for short), is surrounded by a single lipid bilayer. The interior of the endoplasmic reticulum, which is called the **ER lumen**, is filled with a solution that is similar to cytosol. The many folds of the endoplasmic reticulum give it an incredibly extensive surface area, up to 10 square meters (107.6 square feet) of ER in a milliliter of plant cell cytoplasm.[2] Assuming that cytoplasm accounts for about 10% of a plant cell's volume, then one could estimate that an 18-pound watermelon might contain as much as 7,500 square meters of endoplasmic reticulum! That's more than enough ER to cover a college football field. The large, convoluted area allows for a high amount of biochemical activity in a small space. Remember: surface area is an important feature in cells.

Two types of ER are found within a plant cell: **rough ER** and **smooth ER**. The rough ER form flattened sacs, called **cisternae,** that are speckled with ribosomes on the cytosolic surface of their membranes, giving them a bumpy appearance under a microscope. Proteins that are assembled on these ribosomes become either inserted into the ER membrane or injected into the ER lumen. Smooth ER, which has no ribosomes on its surface, usually forms membranous tubes that are thought to connect different regions of the cell like a subway system. Smooth ER is also responsible for producing some of the lipids in a cell (e.g., those found in membranes).

THE GOLGI BODY

Proteins that have been correctly synthesized and folded in or on the rough endoplasmic reticulum may be sent to a protein-processing center called a **Golgi body** for further modification. Golgi bodies are made of five to eight flattened sacs of membranes, called cisternae, which look like a stack of pancakes. Proteins move from one cisterna to the next and are modified into their mature forms. The Golgi body concentrates, packages, and sorts mature proteins into membrane-bound vesicles that carry them to their proper destinations (i.e., the plasma membrane); in this respect, the Golgi bodies act like the postal service of the cell (Figure 2.2). Golgi bodies also produce **polysaccharides** (many sugar molecules linked together) for the cell wall (see Chapter 3).

MITOCHONDRIA: POWERHOUSES OF THE CELL

The energetic requirements of a eukaryotic cell are so high that an internal organelle is present whose sole purpose is to provide a chemical "currency" of energy. These organelles, called **mitochondria** (singular, **mitochondrion**), are the sites of the chemical process **respiration**, whereby sugars and oxygen are used to

Figure 2.2 The endoplasmic reticulum (orange) and Golgi bodies (blue) facilitate the synthesis and sorting of many of the cell's proteins. Ribosomes on the rough ER surface receive mRNAs from the nucleus (center) and synthesize proteins into the ER membrane or ER lumen. These proteins may be sent to the cisternae of the Golgi body for further modification. If a protein is destined for the plasma membrane, then membrane vesicles shuttle it there. Two such vesicles are shown on the right, fusing to the inner surface of the plasma membrane.

produce a large cache of adenosine triphosphate (**ATP**; the energy currency). ATP releases energy when it reacts with many proteins throughout the cell, splitting into adenosine diphosphate (ADP) and an inorganic phosphate molecule. Picture a baseball player against the left field wall with his gloved hand stretched out to catch this ball of energy heading toward the wall. Proteins capture this energy and use it to do work; muscle proteins in animals, as a matter of fact, function by using the stored energy of

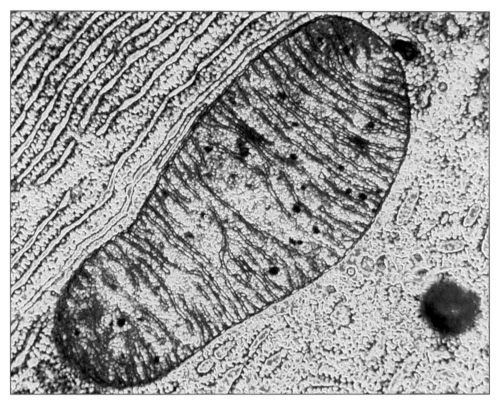

Figure 2.3 Pictured here is a cross-section of a mitochondrion inside a cell. The folds of the inner membrane (cristae) allow greater surface area for respiration. The folded structure outside the mitochondrion (upper left) is rough endoplasmic reticulum, where many of the cell's proteins are made. Mitochondria are in constant motion inside the cell: they move around the cytoplasm rapidly, fusing with one another and dividing.

ATP. A plant cell may contain hundreds or thousands of factory-like mitochondria, depending on its activity.

Mitochondria are small organelles, typically 500 nanometers in diameter (Figure 2.3). Mitochondria are in constant motion inside the cell: they move around the cytoplasm rapidly, fusing with one another and dividing equally as often. Two sets of lipid bilayers surround a mitochondrion: an outer membrane and an inner membrane. The inner membrane is highly folded to

Hot Stinky Flowers

Not all flowers—roses and violets, for example—attract pollinators with sweet fragrances. In fact, some plants, such as aroids and several orchids, take the opposite approach—they imitate the vile stench of a dung heap or a rotting corpse. Many aroids in the Araceae family, which include skunk cabbage and *Amorphophallus titanum* (commonly called the "corpse flower" or titan arum), attract flies and beetles as a means of spreading pollen from one flower to another. These insects, unlike birds and bees, seek to lay their eggs inside carrion or feces rather than looking for a source of nectar or edible pollen. In order to lure such pollinators to their flowers, many species of aroids mimic the properties of decaying animal matter: dark coloration, a putrid odor, and radiation of heat (indicative of active microbial decomposers).

Heat production (thermogenesis) in aroids comes from an alternative metabolic pathway within their mitochondria. A specialized floral structure, called a spadix, which is surrounded by the many small flowers of the plant, contains millions of mitochondria that, like animals, fungi, and other eukaryotes, use the chemical energy of sugars to produce ATP. A plant-specific protein, however, enables the mitochondria to divert that energy from ATP production and release it as heat. This series of reactions can be so effective in some species that they can raise their temperature 20° to 40° C (68° to 104° F) above that of the air around them!

The heat generated by alternative respiration is not wasted energy, but is actually put to good use. The increased temperature evaporates odorant molecules, which reek of decaying flesh or dung, allowing them to waft great distances to potential pollinators. The heat also helps to fool the attracted insects into approaching the pollen-bearing flowers by maintaining the warmth of a decomposing entity. Eastern skunk cabbage, which flowers in early spring, even melts snow as a means of exposing its flowers for pollination from lingering ground cover.

increase its surface area. These folds are known as **cristae**. The space within the inner membrane is called the **mitochondrial matrix**. Within the mitochondrial matrix are DNA molecules that encode a small set of bacteria-like genes. Small ribosomes are also located within the matrix to synthesize mitochondrial proteins from mitochondrial RNA.

Though plant cells contain many of the same cellular features found within other eukaryotic cells, their lifestyle has demanded certain unique additions. The next chapter describes the attributes that, together, make a plant cell differ from the cells of other eukaryotes such as animals or fungi.

3 Unique Features of the Plant Cell

Nature knows no pause in progress and development,
and attaches her curse on all inaction.
— Johann Wolfgang von Goethe

Unique Features of the Plant Cell

Hundreds of millions of years have passed since the ancient ancestor of all eukaryotes lived on this planet. This single-cell organism divided, starting a lineage of offspring that, with time, gave rise to the diverse species we see on Earth today. In this long period of time, plants have become very distinct from other groups of organisms. The **cell wall**, **vacuole**, **plastids**, and **plasmodesmata** are the defining features that make plant cells unique.

THE CELL WALL

The term *plant cell* refers to the sum of two parts: the **protoplast**, which includes the plasma membrane and its contents (cytoplasm, nucleus, cytoskeleton, etc.), and the rigid wall outside of the plasma membrane. This cell wall is a defining characteristic of plant cells (Figure 3.1). Prokaryotes, algae, and fungi also have walls around their cells, though these walls have a different chemical composition than those of plants. Animal cells do not have external walls, but instead build up extensive cytoskeletons within them for structure.

The main scaffolding units of the cell wall are molecules called **cellulose**. At a chemical level, cellulose consists of many sugar units (glucose) linked together by chemical bonds like a chain: many chains wind together with one another to form cellulose **microfibrils** in the same way that many strings twist together to form rope. Microfibrils are 10 nanometers in diameter, stronger than an equivalently sized strand of steel, and are woven together like a cloth around the cell.

Hemicellulose is a class of polysaccharides (chains of simple sugar) found in the cell wall that interconnect cellulose microfibrils. They bind tightly to cellulose and keep neighboring microfibrils together, increasing the strength of the wall in the same way that crossbars reinforce buildings. The bonds between cellulose and hemicelluloses are not permanent and may be broken if the cell wall needs to be modified.

Pectins are gel-like materials that glue neighboring cell walls together. Pectins are found in high concentrations in the layer

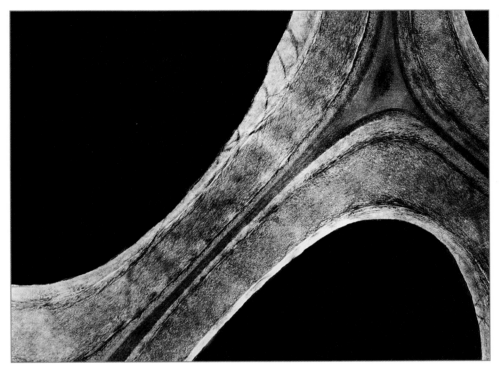

Figure 3.1 The cell wall, made mostly of cellulose, hemicellulose, and pectin, is a defining characteristic of plant cells. Shown here are the walls of three adjacent cells of a Canadian Yew, a type of evergreen tree (magnified 22,000x). The cell wall controls a plant's size and shape.

between adjacent plant cells (called the **middle lamella**); they act like cement, preventing plant cells from falling apart like a tower of marbles. Pectins are so good at gelling that they are added to jams and jellies by the food industry and home canners as thickening and gelling agents.

The most important role of the cell wall is that of support, both for single cells as well as entire plants. The giant redwood trees in California that reach heights in excess of 300 feet are supported almost entirely by the strong cell walls of their trunks. The rigid structure of the wall provides a framework for the entire cell, determining its overall shape like a Jell-O™ mold and limiting its ability to expand. The protoplast is so full of water that it exerts a large, positive force (pressure) against the cell wall. This pressure, called **turgor**, is so great that the protoplast would explode were it not for the cell wall surrounding it. Car tires function in the same manner, allowing the inner tube within to be under pressure without popping. Just as a flat tire cannot support the weight of a car, nonwoody plants cannot support themselves when they do not have enough water to maintain turgor pressure in their cells. This process is known as **wilting**.

The cell wall has various other functions in addition to its structural role. The tough cell walls protect a plant from being eaten by **herbivores** and infectious bacteria. Walls also can serve as food storage units: seeds (which can live for thousands of years) and some fruits are able to break down the sugars in their cell walls and use them for energy. Walls are also important in the transport of water in the root, which will be discussed in Chapter 7.

Humans use the walls of plant cells in countless ways every day. Cell walls function as raw materials to produce many man-made products such as cotton clothing, wood for burning or building, and even paper for the pages in this book. Livestock such as cattle use bacteria to digest cell walls for nutrients (humans cannot), making them an important, indirect source of food. It is nearly impossible for a person to go through a day without using something that is made from plant cell walls.

THE VACUOLE

Mature plant cells appear to consist mostly of empty space when viewed under a microscope, but these "empty spaces" are in fact the fluid-filled organelles known as vacuoles. A vacuole is a large reservoir of water and salts that is surrounded by a single lipid bilayer called the **tonoplast**. The liquid content, called **cell sap**, is highly acidic and is responsible for the sour taste of citrus fruits such as lemons and limes. Young cells, such as those in growing tissues, may contain several smaller vacuoles that, upon maturation, merge into a single, central vacuole that can fill as much as 90% of the cell volume.

The vacuole is more than just a fluid-filled sac; like the cell wall, it serves a host of vital functions in the plant cell. By filling the majority of the protoplast with relatively "inexpensive" cell sap, which requires relatively little energy to make, it allows a plant cell to be quite large without wasting energy synthesizing many proteins and cytoskeletal elements. The vacuole is also a storage container that holds salts, sugars, and organic molecules. Some specialized vacuoles also store one or more of the following:

Pigments: Many red, pink, and blue flower petals get their beautiful colors from water-soluble pigments that are dissolved in the cell sap. Some ornamental leaves also get their coloration in this manner.

Defense compounds: In order to avoid being eaten by animals, fungi, or bacteria, a plant may store poisons, terrible-tasting molecules, and even razor-sharp crystals in its vacuoles.

Toxic chemicals: The vacuole is a safe place to load chemicals that would otherwise damage the rest of the cell. This detoxification function is analogous to how an animal's liver removes poisons from its bloodstream.

The vacuole also breaks down, or recycles, large molecules within a plant cell. In a special process known as **autophagy,** the cell may even digest whole organelles during times of food shortage. Animal cells do not have vacuoles to perform this destructive task and use organelles, called **lysosomes,** instead.

THE PLASTIDS

The plastids are a group of organelles that are unique to plants and algae. They are located in the cytoplasm of every living plant cell. Like mitochondria and the nucleus, plastids have two sets of lipid bilayers surrounding them: an outer membrane and an inner membrane, which are collectively called the **envelope.** Plastids also have their own ribosomes and DNA molecules, which means that in addition to the nucleus and mitochondria, plastids constitute the third of three genomes within a plant cell.

The term *plastid* includes several different subtypes, each with specific functions and characteristics. The different plastids are capable of converting between forms. Three major classes of plastids can be identified based solely on their coloration: chloroplasts (green), chromoplasts (red/orange/yellow), and leucoplasts (no color).

Chloroplasts: Photosynthetic Factories

Chloroplasts are the most abundant plastids found in the above-ground portion of a plant. They are responsible for capturing energy from the sunlight and using it to convert carbon dioxide into sugar (photosynthesis). Chloroplasts look like small, green disks under a microscope (Figure 3.2).

The structure of a chloroplast is somewhat more complicated than that of a mitochondrion. Within the envelope (inner and outer membranes) is a fluid-filled cavity known as the **stroma.** The stroma contains an extensive network of membranes, known as the **thylakoid** membranes, which forms stacks called **grana** (singular, granum). The thylakoid membranes, which surround the fluid-filled cavity, are studded with thousands of photosynthetic proteins and pigments. The primary pigment is **chlorophyll**, the molecule that gives a plant its green color.

Chloroplasts are the only site within a plant cell where photosynthesis may occur. This is because these organelles are specialized to use energy from sunlight to form sugar from atmospheric carbon dioxide. The sugars produced from photosynthesis are sent throughout the plant to be broken down by the mitochondria for energy or stored for later use. In addition to making sugar for

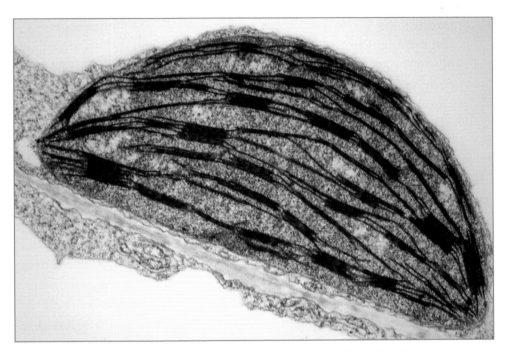

Figure 3.2 Chloroplasts are the most abundant plastids found in the aboveground portion of a plant and are responsible for photosynthesis. Shown here is a microscopic view of a chloroplast from a leaf of a tobacco plant. The dark green, threadlike structures are cholorphyll-containing thylakoid membranes, which convert the Sun's energy into chemical energy. The regions of the thylakoid membrane that look like stacks of coins are grana.

the plant, chloroplasts also make some amino acids and lipids. Plant cells could not survive without chloroplasts because they would not be able to make their own food (with the exception of some parasitic plant species).

Chromoplasts: Advertisements for Animals

Red bell peppers, orange carrots, and the yellow flowers of butter-cups have something in common: they all get their colors from **chromoplasts**. Chromoplasts are structurally similar to chloroplasts except that instead of containing chlorophyll, they are full of **carotenoids**. Carotenoids are the pigments that are responsible for the variety of reds, oranges, and yellows seen in plant tissues (Figure 3.3). **Carotene** is a common carotenoid and is the source of vitamin A in our diets. Many ripe fruits and fertile flowers convert their chloroplasts into chromoplasts as a means of attracting pollinating and seed-dispersing animals.

Photosynthetic Sea Slugs

The oceans of our world are home to great wonders, including animals that can photosynthesize. Though plants, algae, and cyanobacteria are the dominant photoautotrophs of the planet, a group of marine sea slugs (nudibranchs) have capitalized on the ability to harvest the sun's energy for food.

Mollusks in the order Ascoglossa, which have no protective shell, are particularly susceptible to being eaten by predators as they forage in marine waters throughout the globe. As a protective measure, many species have evolved a unique way of blending in with the very algae on which they feed. Using a special tooth-like organ, the sea slugs puncture a hole in filaments of siphonous green algae from which they suck out the contents. Instead of eating the algae, however, the invertebrate discards all of the cellular matter except for the chloroplasts; these are incorporated into the cells lining its digestive tract. These cells, which are highly branched and lie only one cell layer below the mollusk's epidermis, receive outside light and are visible from the animal's exterior.

The benefit of "stealing" chloroplasts from algae has been the focus of many studies over the past decades. Visually, chloroplasts help to camouflage the sea slug from potential predators. Amazingly, the naked chloroplasts within the animal cells remain alive and functional for up to several months, fixing carbon dioxide into sugar and releasing oxygen. These sugars are enough to sustain the sea slug for months in the absence of any food. The fixed carbon is also used to build defensive chemicals and slimy mucus for protection.

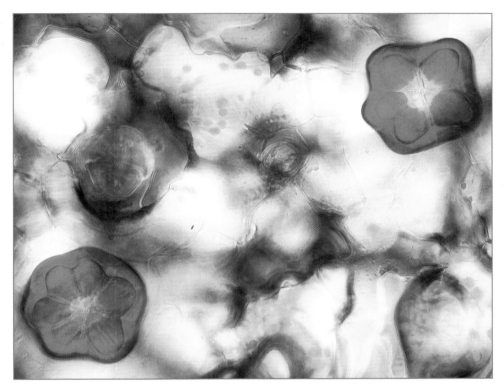

Figure 3.3 Chromoplasts, such as these from a magnified Begonia petal, are plastids lacking chlorophyll but rich in carotenoids. Carotenoids are pigments that lend a yellow, orange, or red hue to some plant cells.

Leucoplasts: Colorless Plastids with Variable Functions

Plastids that have no coloration at all are referred to as **leucoplasts**. One type of leucoplast, called an **amyloplast**, accumulates in storage tissues such as potato tubers and cereal grains (e.g., wheat, rice, corn). These plastids are responsible for converting the products of photosynthesis (simple sugars) into large **starch** molecules (chains of repeatedly-linked glucose molecules) for long-term food storage. Amyloplasts create so much starch that it crystallizes to form large granules within the double-membrane. The weight of these plastids in cells indicates to the root which way is down, making them essential for proper gravity perception. Studies using mutant plants that are incapable of making starch have revealed roots with severely reduced sensitivity to gravity: when these roots are placed sideways, they barely bend downward (Figure 3.4).

Other leucoplasts have different functions, ranging from protein storage to fat synthesis. A unique leucoplast found in specialized cells of *Cecropia peltata* (the tropical "trumpet-tree") makes the chemical **glycogen** instead of starch. Glycogen, which is the animal equivalent of starch (also a polymer of glucose), has no apparent use within the plant, but serves as food for a colony of ants that lives on its surface. By providing glycogen for ants, the plant gains protection from herbivores; the six-legged inhabitants immediately attack any animal that tries to eat their home and food source.

PLASMODESMATA

When multicellular organisms evolved from their respective unicellular ancestors, they required a physical link that would allow continuity between the individual cells. A successful multicellular organism needs connections between cells because they permit cell-to-cell communication as well as the intercellular trafficking of **metabolites**, ions, micromolecules, and macromolecules (such as RNA and proteins). In response to this need, fungi developed pores between cells, animals evolved structures known as gap junctions, and plants formed plasmodesmata (singular, plasmodesma). Plasmodesmata are tiny, membrane-lined channels that traverse the walls of two cells, thereby connecting them. The significance of such connections is quite profound: the cytoplasm of many individual protoplasts is, in fact, continuous!

There are two types of these channels that differ largely in origin only: **primary plasmodesmata** and **secondary plasmodesmata**. Primary plasmodesmata form during the division of one mother cell into two daughter cells (see Chapter 4) and actually trap ER

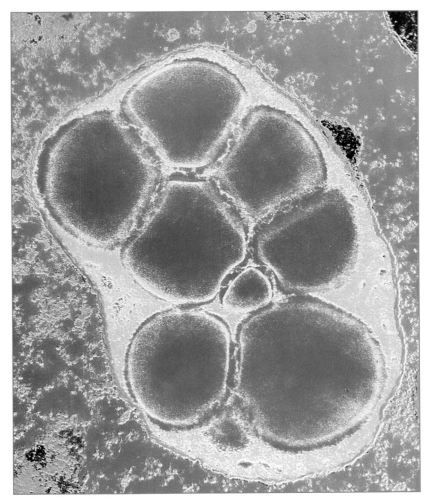

Figure 3.4 Amyloplasts, like this one from an onion (magnified 18,000x), convert the simple sugars from photosynthesis into large starch molecules for long-term food storage. The starch becomes so concentrated that it crystallizes into large granules (shown in blue) within the double membrane.

within them. The strand of ER is shared by the two neighboring cells and is called the **desmotubule** because it forms a tube within the plasmodesma. Secondary plasmodesmata form between mature cells by restructuring part of the cell walls and fusing the membranes of the two adjacent cells together. Microscopic observations have revealed that clusters of many plasmodesmata occur in certain cell types.

Plasmodesmata function as a filter of sorts, allowing selective passage between adjacent cells. The inner diameter of the channel is so packed with endoplasmic reticulum and proteins that spaces only a few nanometers in diameter are left for movement. These spaces, which are thousands of times smaller than the width of a human hair, are sufficient for water, charged atoms, and very small cytoplasmic molecules to pass freely between cells while larger molecules are excluded. When a transported item (such as water or a virus) moves from cell to cell through plasmodesmata, then its movement is called

Cellular Slaves

Many genetic, biochemical, and microscopic data, along with fossil evidence, suggest that mitochondria and plastids descended from free-living prokaryotes that were incorporated into the cell. It is thought that the common ancestor of all eukaryotes engulfed a single bacterium over 1.5 billion years ago, which persisted within the host, and evolved into the mitochondria of today. At least 300 million years later (~1.2 billion years ago), some of these mitochondria-containing eukaryotes engulfed another prokaryote, this time a photosynthetic cyanobacterium. This occurrence, called an endosymbiotic event (*endosymbiosis* literally means, "living together within"), created the plastids of modern algae and plants.

Descendants of the original, incorporated prokaryotes have undergone dramatic alterations and reductions to become the organelles of today. Both types of organelles (plastids and mitochondria) have two sets of lipid bilayers surrounding them: the inner membrane is left over from the original prokaryote and the outer membrane formed around the organelle when the host cell engulfed it. The bacterial genomes have gradually been reduced,

symplastic. Some neighboring cells are without plasmodesmata while others have theirs plugged, but the collection of cells that are connected by functional plasmodesmata is referred to as a **symplastic domain.**

An interesting characteristic of plasmodesmata is their dynamic ability to increase their **pore size** (the width of the opening). In an attempt to understand how the relatively large **tobacco mosaic virus** (**TMV**) could spread from cell to cell in infected plants, scientists discovered that the viruses were actually opening the plasmodesmata by producing a special protein. The key-like protein, which is thought to be similar to proteins that plants make, has been found to open the pores of plasmodesmata by several times its original size.

possible only because many of the genes have been relocated to the host nucleus. Nuclear genes that have moved from the mitochondria or plastids encode proteins that are synthesized in the cytosol and must be transported to their specific target organelle.

Additional examples of endosymbiotic events have taken place in the last several million years; these are called secondary endosymbiosis. Secondary endosymbiosis occurs when a nonphotosynthetic eukaryote engulfs an alga and maintains it as a plastid. Plastids that are acquired by secondary endosymbiosis often have more than two membranes (usually three or four) and may sometimes contain a remnant of the algal nucleus.

The captive organelles of eukaryotes have, over time, lost their ability to survive outside of their host cell; for this reason, plastids and mitochondria are known as semi-autonomous organelles. Though they have become biochemical workhorses for the host cell, these descendants of free-living bacteria are not without their benefits: in return for respiration or photosynthesis, the organelles are awarded the luxuries of a eukaryotic lifestyle.

The flower is the poetry of reproduction.
It is an example of the eternal seductiveness of life.

— Jean Giraudoux,
The Enchantment, 1933

Cell Division

All of the plants on this planet, from the smallest mosses to the tallest trees, begin their lives as single cells. That first cell duplicates itself to become two cells and then four cells and then eight cells and so on, each with identical copies of DNA in their nuclei. In the case of very large plants, which can consist of hundreds of billions of cells, it is remarkable that this process can proceed with so few mistakes. Cells duplicate, allowing tiny seeds to become large plants. A second type of division process introduces genetic variability and leads to sexual reproduction.

Growth is an irreversible increase in size and is the result of two processes, **cell division** and **cell enlargement**. In cell division, a single cell splits in two, doubling the number of cells. Though these divisions create more cells in an organism, they do not, by themselves, increase the size of the organism. Almost all of the growth in a plant's volume comes from the enlargement of its cells.

There are specific locations in a plant body where cell division occurs. These regions, called **meristems**, consist of **undifferentiated** cells that are general and have no special structures. Meristems produce **primary meristems** that divide into specialized tissues. Meristems also regenerate themselves so that they may continue to create new cells indefinitely. This type of growth is called **indeterminate growth** because, in theory, it will not end during the lifetime of the plant.

THE CELL CYCLE: INTERPHASE AND MITOSIS

Dividing cells undergo a series of changes in order to properly duplicate themselves. The discrete phases and checkpoints of this process repeat for each division and are collectively referred to as the **cell cycle**. The cell cycle consists of two major phases, **interphase** and **mitosis.** Most of a cell's growth, metabolic activity, and lifetime occur in interphase, while mitosis—the process of cell division—is a relatively short cycle lasting only hours. Interphase is further subdivided into three phases: two gap phases (G_1 and G_2) separated by a DNA duplication event (**S phase**).

INTERPHASE

The first stage of interphase, G_1, is highly active. During G_1, the cell doubles in size in preparation for its upcoming reduction that will occur during mitosis. The ER synthesizes additional membranous organelles (Golgi body, vacuole); plastids and mitochondria double in number; and protein synthesis of cytoskeletal elements, enzymes, and ribosomes increases. In addition to growth, the cell also begins to rearrange itself. The nucleus migrates to the center of the cell, often suspended in the vacuole by strands of cytoplasm. These strands converge and fuse, forming a sheet that divides the vacuole into two halves. This sheet, called the **phragmosome,** is the first physical division that occurs within the cell. Once all of the necessary changes have been made, the cell proceeds into the next stage of interphase, the S phase. However, if something has not occurred properly, then the cell must first adjust before continuing to the S phase. When the cell passes this regulation point, known as the **G_1 checkpoint**, it is committed to cell division.

Following the G_1 phase of interphase, the cell enters S phase in which the genetic contents of the cell are duplicated. Each DNA molecule within the nucleus replicates itself so that there are two identical copies. Not only is it critical that every DNA molecule gets copied only once, but it is also crucial that few or no mistakes are made in the process. To appreciate the magnitude of such a task, consider that the entire genome of *Arabidopsis thaliana*, a common plant used in laboratories, contains between 115 million and 125 million base pairs, which is a relatively small number when compared to other species. Duplicating the genome of one *Arabidopsis* cell would be like trying to copy this book 1,000 times without making an error!

Once the genetic material in the nucleus has been completely replicated, the cell proceeds to the final stage of interphase, G_2. The cell begins to assemble structures that will be used in division, and the DNA molecules of the nucleus begin to condense.

Microscopic studies have revealed that during G_2, a ring of microtubules forms around the center of the cell, creating what is called the **preprophase band.** A visible feature of the G_2 phase, the preprophase band is now recognized to be a critical component of proper cell division. Mutant plants that form inappropriately-oriented preprophase bands divide incorrectly. The **G_2 checkpoint** is the final stage at the end of interphase to ensure that all of the necessary preparations have been made before the cell progresses into mitosis; if any one aspect is not right, then it must first be amended before advancing.

MITOSIS

Mitosis is the process of creating two genetically identical nuclei from the existing nucleus of the dividing cell. The series of events that lead to the equal partitioning of duplicated DNA into new nuclei are divided into four major phases: **prophase, metaphase, anaphase,** and **telophase.**

Prophase

The first stage of mitosis, prophase, involves major changes to the nucleus and its contents. The duplicated DNA molecules—which are distributed throughout the nucleus like long, tangled strings—begin to coil and condense into shorter, thicker packages. When viewed under a microscope, the DNA appears first as long threads, then discrete objects, and then, finally, as **chromosomes.** Chromosomes consist of two identical DNA molecules, called **sister chromatids,** which had been duplicated during the replication of the S phase. These linear, coiled molecules are joined at their centers by a special sequence of DNA, known as a **centromere;** the resulting structure of a chromosome looks much like an "X" (Figure 4.1).

As the DNA within the nucleus finishes condensing into chromosomes, the surrounding nuclear envelope begins to degrade. At the same time, microtubules begin to surround the

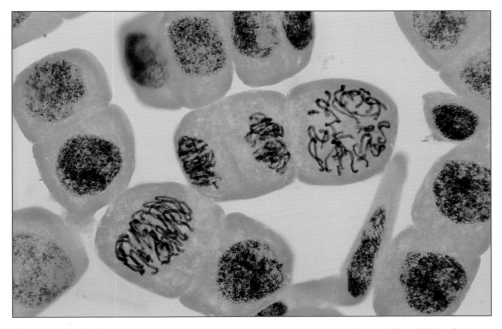

Figure 4.1 Cells from an onion root tip are undergoing mitosis. The DNA of these cells, stained blue, is present as either diffuse chromatin or as condensed chromosomes (center).

deteriorating nucleus. The sudden disappearance of the envelope demarcates the transition between prophase and the next stage of mitosis: metaphase.

Metaphase

During the second phase of mitosis, known as metaphase, the chromosomes that are released from the nucleus during prophase are aligned in the center of the cell where division will occur. This movement is accomplished with the help of microtubules and molecular motors.

When the nuclear envelope breaks down at the end of prophase, the chromosomes are suddenly exposed to many new proteins. Long filaments of microtubules, called the **mitotic spindle**, form a cage where the nucleus used to be. The filaments, which consist of bundles of microtubules known as **spindle fibers,** radiate from two poles known as **microtubule organizing centers** (analagous or similar to the centrosomes in animals). The combination of a microtubule organizing center and its spindle fibers is known as an **aster,** of which there are two in a dividing cell. The spindle fibers oscillate their growth, elongating and shrinking like a choreographed, cytological dance. Protein complexes known as **kinetochores,** which are bound to the centromeres of each sister chromatid, grab onto an elongating microtubule, attaching the chromosome. Once a spindle fiber is attached to a kinetochore, it becomes a **kinetochore microtubule.** Spindle fibers that do not attach to kinetochores are known as **polar microtubules.** Polar microtubules become so long that the spindle fibers of the two microtubule organizing centers overlap in the middle of the cell.

A chromosome that is attached through a kinetochore to the mitotic spindle begins to move toward the pole due to the degradation (shortening) of the microtubules by kinetochore proteins. As it migrates, however, the kinetochore on the opposite centromere attaches to a spindle fiber from the other aster. Given that the two kinetochore microtubules exert equal forces in opposite directions, the net result is a tug-of-war that ends in a tie: all of the chromosomes in the cell end up in the middle of the cell, aligned in a row exactly halfway between the two poles. Once this alignment is complete, metaphase is officially over and the next phase, anaphase, begins.

Anaphase

When all chromosomes are lined up in the middle of the cell, a rapid and visually distinct phase of mitosis begins: anaphase. In some dividing cells, anaphase may last as little as 2 minutes, making this phase difficult to observe in living cells. Anaphase officially begins when the paired centromeres of each sister chromatid in a chromosome separate from one another, severing the only bond that was keeping them together. Once this detachment has occurred, the chromatids drift apart toward the opposite poles, since they are still attached to the kinetochore microtubules. The driving force of this movement comes not only from microtubule disassembly, but also from molecular motors that push the overlapping polar microtubules apart from one another. The chromatids move so fast that the arms on each side of the centromere drag through the cytoplasm and form a "V" shape that points at the pole. When separation is complete and each pole receives one copy of each DNA molecule, then anaphase is complete.

Telophase

At the beginning of telophase, each end of the cell contains one identical copy of each chromosome and the cell begins to revert back to its interphase form. The mitotic spindle dissociates and degrades, freeing tubulin subunits for other microtubule functions in the cell. The DNA, which is still tightly coiled and condensed, begins to unwind and uncoil. As the DNA molecules unfurl, vesicles fuse around them to form new nuclear envelopes. Once the new nuclei, or **daughter nuclei**, are complete, then telophase and mitosis ends (Figure 4.2).

Cytokinesis: Dividing the Cytoplasm with a New Cell Wall

In most plant cells, mitosis is followed closely by **cytokinesis**, the division of one cell into two. Cytokinesis in plant cells is almost completely different from that in animals. Animal cells divide by constricting the middle with an external ring of actin micro-filaments. Plant cells, on the other hand, create a new cell wall from inside that divides the protoplast in two.

During telophase, once the mitotic spindle has disassembled, a barrel-shaped array of microtubules, called the **phragmoplast,** forms between the maturing daughter nuclei. Phragmoplasts in dividing cells serve as highways for molecular motors to move along, carrying vesicles toward the middle. The vesicles, which

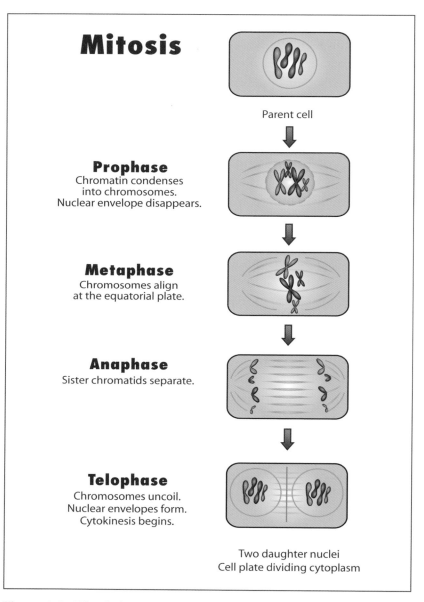

Figure 4.2 Mitosis is the process of creating two genetically identical nuclei from the existing nucleus of the dividing cell. The series of events that lead to the equal partitioning of duplicated DNA into new nuclei are divided into four major phases: prophase, metaphase, anaphase, and telophase.

arise from the Golgi body, contain cell wall materials such as pectins and hemicelluloses. As these vesicular cargoes are delivered to the center of the cell, they fuse together to form a windowed sheet of membrane-bound cell wall. This sheet, called the **cell plate**, expands outward to the edges of the cell. The windows begin to close, trapping strands of ER that later form the desmotubules of plasmodesmata (see Chapter 3).

When the cell plate reaches the periphery of the cell mid-section, its membrane fuses with the lipid bilayer of the plasma membrane: each surface of the cell plate membrane becomes continuous with the plasma membrane of one of the two daughter cells. A consequence of this fusion—in addition to the formation of two protoplasts from one—is that the cell wall materials inside the cell plate become the layer that divides the two daughter cells, merging with the existing cell wall. The merger of cell plate and plasma membrane marks the end of cytokinesis and the end of cell division. In place of the single mother cell, two daughter cells exist!

MEIOSIS

With the exception of identical twins, human siblings often look quite different from one another; although they share the same parents, their hair color, eye color, height, and other such traits may vary. The genetic variability among the offspring of two parents—whether they are people, pachyderms, or petunias—can be traced to a special form of cell division called **meiosis**. Meiosis, which occurs only in sexual structures (e.g., flowers), mixes up an individual's genes into many combinations such that, statistically, each of its offspring will be different. Genetic variability is often advantageous; the parent cannot predict what conditions the future will bring and an assortment of offspring helps to ensure that at least one will survive to reproduce again.

In meiotic cell division, a mother cell divides twice to generate four genetically distinct daughter cells, each with exactly half of the original number of chromosomes. In animals, these daughter cells are called **gametes** and are the sperm and egg cells that fuse to form a **zygote**. By contrast, plant meiosis produces **spores** that

Galls: Plant Tumors

Cancer develops in animals when cells lose control of their otherwise highly regulated cell cycle. Cancerous cells often divide rapidly to form an abnormal growth called a tumor, which may become life threatening. Tumor-like structures called galls are found throughout the plant kingdom.

Galls, unlike tumors, usually form in response to a second organism, often a parasite. Many life-forms have been found to cause galls, including viruses, bacteria, insects, fungi, nematodes, and mites. These organisms may alter the host plant's cell division pattern either through DNA modification or through chemical signals, resulting in the formation of enlarged structures (galls) where they may proliferate or lay eggs. Thus, the plant cells are used to house and nourish the pathogen.

Gall form is almost as diverse as the number of species that cause them. They may occur on any part of the plant (e.g., root, stem, leaf, flower, fruit), or they may form an entirely new organ. Some of the more fantastic galls have been described as looking like berries, nuts, fungi, sea urchins, and grotesquely developed horns or clubs.

Cecidology, the study of plant galls, may be traced back thousands of years and proves to remain useful today. Many crops, notably fruit trees, suffer from a variety of galls. The biotech industry has benefited from the understanding of a soil bacterium, *Agrobacterium tumefaciens*, which enters ground-level plant wounds and causes the crown gall and hairy root diseases. The bacterium injects some of its own DNA into the host cells, overriding their normal function and causing them to divide rapidly into a resulting gall. Scientists have taken advantage of this natural genetic engineer and used it as a means to insert foreign DNA into plants; most genetically modified plants have been transformed in this manner.

must divide by mitosis to produce gametes (also sperm and eggs). In both plants and animals, the phases of meiosis are the same. The two divisions, called meiosis I and meiosis II, both contain a prophase, a metaphase, an anaphase, and a telophase (Figure 4.3).

Prophase I

The shuffling of genes along each chromosome occurs during prophase I, which leads to genetic variability between the resulting daughter cells. In prophase I, as in the prophase of mitosis, the DNA condenses into chromosomes, each made of two identical sister chromatids. Two sets of chromosomes are present in the nucleus, one set inherited from each parent. Potatoes, for instance, have 46 chromosomes: 23 from each parent. Each chromosome has a partner of equivalent size and contains similar hereditary information (genes). Such partners are called **homologous chromosomes.** Homologous chromosomes pair together and exchange portions of DNA with each other by physically breaking and reforming the DNA molecules. This process, called **crossing over**, is unique to prophase I. Once the genetic material has been exchanged between homologous chromosomes and the nuclear envelope breaks down, prophase I ends and metaphase I begins.

Metaphase I

Metaphase I is similar to the metaphase of mitosis except for the final arrangement of the chromosomes. In mitosis, the chromosomes align in the center of the cell in a single line such that the sister chromatids split from each other. In metaphase I, however, each homologous pair lines up along the division plane together, one on each side.

An important feature of metaphase I that contributes to genetic variability during meiosis is the random assortment of homologous chromosomes along the division plane. The chromosome

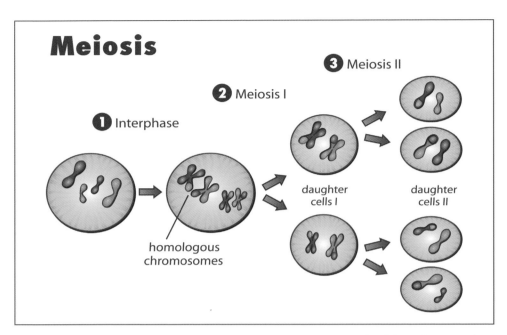

Figure 4.3 Meiosis, in both plants and animals, mixes up an individual's genes into many combinations so that each of its offspring will be different. In meiotic cell division, a mother cell divides twice to generate four genetically distinct daughter cells, each with exactly half of the original number of chromosomes. The two divisions, called meiosis I and meiosis II, both contain a prophase, a metaphase, an anaphase, and a telophase stage.

sets that were inherited from the mother (maternal) and father (paternal) plants are similar but not identical. There is no preference as to which side of the cell the maternal chromosomes will reside at the end of metaphase I. Likewise, there is no preference as to which side of the cell the paternal chromosomes will end up. Thus, at the end of metaphase I, each side of the cell most likely will contain a random assortment of maternal and paternal chromosomes that, together, constitute a complete set.

Anaphase I

Anaphase I is mechanistically identical to mitotic anaphase. The spindle microtubules haul their cargo to their respective poles on each end of the cell. The difference from mitosis, however, arises from the alternative orientation of the homologous chromosomes in metaphase I. Both poles receive one homologue from each homologous pair rather than identical sister chromatids from all chromosomes.

Again, it is important to highlight the effect of random assortment during the first meiotic division. Following anaphase I, each end of the dividing cell contains a complete set of genes, though these are derived from a combination of maternal and paternal genes.

Telophase I

Telophase I proceeds as in mitosis. New nuclear envelopes form around the uncoiling chromosomes. The spindle also breaks down at this time. It is important to reiterate that the daughter nuclei in telophase I are genetically distinct, due to the contributions of crossing over and random assortment. Telophase I is often followed by cytokinesis.

Meiosis II

Most meiotically dividing cells move directly into prophase II from telophase I. DNA replication does not occur between these steps. The two daughter cells from meiosis I may be seen undergoing meiosis II in tandem. In prophase II, the DNA molecules again condense and the nuclear envelopes break down. In metaphase II, the chromosomes line up along the equatorial plane, as in mitotic metaphase, with their centromeres in the center. Anaphase II separates the sister chromatids, which are pulled to opposite ends of the cell. Nuclear envelopes form during telophase II, and the chromosomes uncoil. The result, following cytokinesis, is four genetically different daughter cells (spores), each with exactly half of the number of chromosomes that were present in the mother cell.

5 Plant Tissues

Beauty of whatever kind, in its supreme development,
invariably excites the sensitive soul to tears.
— Edgar Allan Poe

Plant Tissues

Multicellular organisms have evolved from unicellular ancestors multiple times over the past billion years, so it should not be surprising that a body of two or more cells provides several advantages. One advantage that muticellularity offers is **specialization,** or adaptation to a particular function or environment. Specialization increases the efficiency of an organism in terms of its ability to survive and reproduce. Examples of specialization exist on many different scales: certain cells are specialized for photosynthesis; some tissues are specialized for protection; whole organs, such as roots, are even specialized for plant anchorage and water/nutrient uptake. On an even higher level, there is specialization in human societies; division of community laborers into bakers, farmers, bankers, and other professions make life easier than if each person had to do everything himself or herself. The resounding theme from living systems is that having many specialized parts working together—especially on a cellular scale—pays off!

Genetically identical cells in a multicellular organism become specialized through **differentiation.** Differentiated cells have distinct structural or biochemical properties from other cells in the plant body. These differences are accomplished by preferentially expressing certain genes and, therefore, synthesizing a unique collection of proteins. As mentioned previously, a collection of cells that have differentiated in a similar fashion and act together to perform a specific function is called a tissue. Tissues in plants further aggregate into larger units known as **tissue systems**, which share function, continuity, and meristematic precursor cells. Plant bodies are composed of three major tissue systems: the **dermal tissue system**, the **ground tissue system,** and the **vascular tissue system.**

DERMAL TISSUE SYSTEM

The dermal tissue system surrounds the entire plant, both above and below ground, and is kind of like a plant's skin. Like skin, its primary function is protection, but the dermal tissues have additional functions that differ depending on whether they surround the root or the shoot. Belowground, the surface cells of the root bridge the interior of a plant and the water in the soil, facilitating the uptake of water and nutrients from the environment. Aboveground, however, the shoot needs to keep the water inside from evaporating uncontrollably. This task also is accomplished by the dermal tissue system. Thus, dermal tissues function in both the uptake of water in the root as well as in the retention of water in the shoot, two seemingly opposite roles.

Two dermal tissues make up the dermal tissue system, the **epidermis** and the **periderm**. The epidermis, which develops from a primary meristem called the **protoderm,** is the only dermal tissue of the plant unless secondary growth occurs. If secondary growth (lateral thickening) occurs, as it does in many stems and roots, then the periderm takes the place and function of the epidermis (see Chapter 6). In shoots, the epidermis may be a single layer of cells or, in the case of plants living in dry environments (i.e., a desert), several layers thick. Most epidermal cells are relatively indistinct, lack chloroplasts, and are coated with a layer of wax called the **cuticle.** This wax keeps water inside the plant and helps rainwater and dew run off of leaves. Wax is also found in abundance on some fruits because it keeps them crisp, full of water, and desirable to eat; this wax is why rubbing an apple causes it to shine.

GROUND TISSUE SYSTEM

Ground tissue makes up the bulk of most nonwoody plants. The ground tissue system develops from the **ground meristem** into three different tissues: **parenchyma, collenchyma,** and **sclerenchyma.**

Parenchyma

Parenchyma tissue is found throughout the plant body. Parenchyma cells are thin-walled and irregularly shaped, and lack

distinct structural or biochemical features. As a result of such com-
monality, cells from many origins fall into the catchall category of
parenchyma. The bulk in most plants is credited to parenchyma
cells because their volume fills the majority of most nonwoody
organs. The center of stems, the photosynthetic portion of leaves,
and the periphery (excluding the epidermis) of roots are all
parenchyma tissues (Figure 5.1). The fleshy parts of most fruits
and vegetables in human diets are also examples of parenchyma.

Parenchyma cells, which are alive at maturity, serve a range of
functions beyond mere space fillers. They act as storage units for
simple sugars (as evident in a sweet apple) and starch (potatoes
are mostly starchy parenchyma), and they are the dominant sites
of photosynthesizing chloroplasts in leaves. Furthermore, they
retain the meristematic ability to differentiate, making them
important cells for wound healing and regeneration.

Collenchyma

Collenchyma tissue usually occurs as bundles just below the
epidermis of stems and petioles (leaf stalks). Collenchyma cells
are surrounded by thick, irregularly shaped **primary cell walls**,
which are relatively flexible and elastic while still supportive. The
characteristics of their pectin-rich cell walls make collenchyma
well suited for structure and support in regions of a plant that
are still elongating: the cells are strong, yet they do not restrict
growth or break in the process. The strings of celery stalks, which
people often find stuck between their teeth, are composed almost
entirely of collenchyma (Figure 5.2). Collenchyma cells, like
parenchyma cells, are typically alive at maturity.

Sclerenchyma

Sclerenchyma cells add strength to plant parts that are no longer
elongating. Unlike collenchyma cells that need to be flexible,
sclerenchyma cells have thick **secondary cell walls**, comprised
mostly of a compound called **lignin** (the cell wall material that

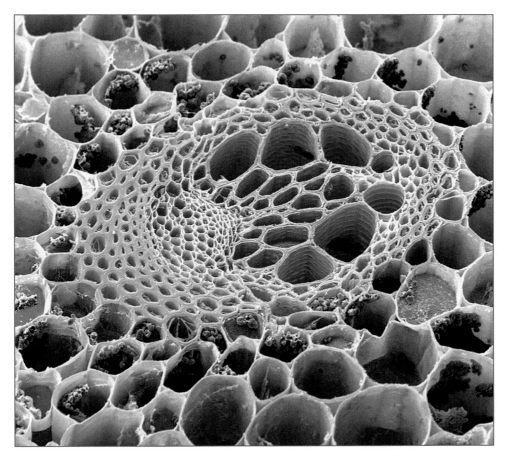

Figure 5.1 Parenchyma tissue is found throughout the plant body. Parenchyma cells are thin-walled and irregularly shaped, and lack distinct structural or biochemical features. In this magnified cross-section of a buttercup stem is an oval vascular bundle embedded in parenchyma cells.

makes wood hard and supportive). Secondary cell walls are deposited inside the primary cell walls by the plasma membrane once the cell is finished elongating. The thick layer of lignin-rich wall material surrounding these cells gives sclerenchyma tissues tremendous strengthening ability. In fact, the Greek word *skleros*, from which we get the word *sclerenchyma*, means "hard." Most sclerenchyma cells, unlike collenchyma and

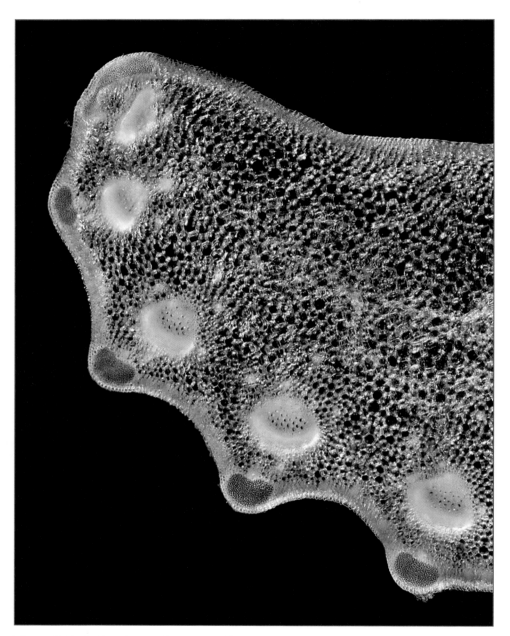

Figure 5.2 Collenchyma tissue usually occurs as bundles just below the epidermis of stems and petioles (leaf stalks). The strings of celery stalks are composed almost entirely of collenchyma.

parenchyma cells, die upon reaching maturity, but their hard cell walls remain in the plant body and continue to function long after the protoplast aborts. There are two main types of sclerenchyma found in plants: **fibers** and **sclereids.**

Fibers are very long, narrow cells with thick secondary walls. They usually occur in bundles, strengthening a plant organ in the way a rebar reinforces concrete. Typical diameters range from 100 to 1,000 micrometers, though many fiber cells are over 10 centimeters in length (recall that there are 10,000 micrometers in a centimeter). This unique physical property makes fiber cells a valuable tool for humans. Hemp fibers from *Cannabis sativa* have long been used for ropes and textiles and were once the major material for ship sails. Flax (*Linum usitatissimum)* fibers, which have virtually no lignin in their thick walls, are currently used in fine fabrics (linen), papers (such as cigarette paper), and even money (U.S. paper notes contain 25% flax fibers, 75% cotton[3]) because of their durable, flexible properties.

Sclereids are a diverse type of sclerenchyma cells found in many plants. These cells are variable in shape and often branched. They may be either scattered throughout a tissue, or clustered together. The gritty texture of pear fruits, for instance, comes from the presence of clusters of tiny sclereids, called stone cells. Sclereids also toughen the coats of many seeds, the stones of fruits such as peaches and the hard, stony exteriors of nuts. Interestingly, the sclereids of ground nutshells, such as those of walnuts, are used as abrasives for cleaning jet engines and enhancing certain cosmetics.

VASCULAR TISSUE SYSTEM

As plants have evolved to become larger, allocation of resources has become an increasingly large problem. A 300-foot-tall tree must move water from the deepest root to the highest leaf; likewise, the sugars made from photosynthesis must be carried from the sunlit leaves all the way down to the subterranean root cells for storage and metabolism. The internal transport of water, nutrients, and sugars is accomplished by the two vascular tissues of the plant body. Water conduction occurs in **xylem** tissue, while food (sugars) is conducted through the **phloem** tissue. Both xylem and phloem arise from the differentiation of **procambium**, the meristematic precursor to vascular tissue.

Xylem: The Water-conducting Cells

Xylem tissue is the major water conducting system in all vascular plants. Xylem includes parenchyma cells for storage and fibers for support, but the majority of xylem consists of conductive cells called **tracheary elements**. Tracheary elements, which are dead at maturity, are one-way streets for water to travel from the roots (where it is absorbed) through the stem and up to the leaves. Structurally, tracheary elements are typically long, narrow tubes with perforations that allow lateral water conduction; essentially, they are like dead, leaky pipes. Water that evaporates from the leaves draws a column of liquid up through the xylem with a tremendous amount of negative pressure (tension). Because of this, tracheary elements have highly lignified walls that prevent the elements from collapsing under this tension in much the way a submarine must be reinforced to resist crumpling while underwater.

Two principal types of tracheary elements exist within vascular plants: **tracheids** and **vessel elements**. Gymnosperms (such as conifer trees) and some flowering plants contain only tracheids, which are long and narrow "pipes." Tracheids are distinct in that water must pass through pairs of **bordered pits** (interruptions of the secondary cell wall) in order to cross from one cell to another. Vessel elements, the dominant tracheary element of angiosperms, are somewhat shorter, wider, and degrade much (or all) of their adjoining end walls to form an essentially continuous, perforated tube called a **vessel**. Vessel elements in angiosperms allow for more rapid translocation of water than tracheids for the same reason that it is faster to drive on the freeway than through town: there are fewer stop signs (pits) to slow traffic (water flow) and more lanes (wider passages).

Two types of xylem are found within a single plant, which fall within two categories: **protoxylem** and **metaxylem.** Protoxylem is xylem that differentiates during elongation, while metaxylem is xylem that differentiates after elongation has finished. The entire cell wall of metaxylem vessel elements are highly lignified and perforated in order to withstand the tension the evaporating water column creates. Protoxylem vessel elements, on the other hand, adopt a different pattern for depositing their secondary cell wall. Cells in an elongating organ must be able to stretch, or they would rip apart as the plant grows. In order to function as water vessels while preventing stretch-induced damage, the lignified walls of protoxylem vessel elements are either **helical** (like a spring) or **annular** (a series of rings): this way the vessels may elongate without breaking and, at the same time, prevent collapsing.

Phloem: The Sugar/Nutrient Transporters

Phloem tissue, which contains several cell types, is specialized to transport the products of photosynthesis (sugars) throughout the plant body. Phloem contains fibers and parenchyma, but the distinguishing characters of this tissue are its conductive cells (Figure 5.3).

The movement of dissolved sugars, called the **phloem sap,** occurs in cells called **sieve tube elements.** These long, narrow cells are stacked end-to-end in columns called **sieve tubes.** The walls of sieve tube elements are perforated with pores and connected with large, plasmodesma-like strands such that their cytoplasm is continuous, linking the cytoplasm of multiple sieve tube elements into a single, large cytoplasm. Perforated plates, located at the upper and lower ends of elements within a sieve tube, are called **sieve plates.**

Sweet Xylem Sap

In early springtime, billows of steam are seen rising from sugarhouses all across the Northeastern United States and Canada. The gaseous water of these clouds is derived from boiled tree sap, leaving sweet, golden syrup that is perfect for pouring over a stack of pancakes. People have enjoyed the sap of sugar maples for several hundred years, taking advantage of their xylem properties.

Sugar maples (*Acer saccharum*) drop their leaves in autumn and rely on stores of starch as a food source in their absence. Beginning in late fall and lasting into spring, the tree's starch reserves are degraded into smaller sugar molecules (sucrose) for distribution throughout the plant. During this leafless period, sucrose levels in the xylem sap range from 1% to 4% by weight.

Sugar makers drill holes into the sapwood of maple tree trunks as winter retreats into spring, collecting the sap that flows out in pails or plastic tubing. The sap that exudes from these "tap holes" during the daytime comes from the roots as well as the trunk and branches. The flow of maple sap is outward because the xylem contents are under greater pressure than the atmosphere (think which way air moves when you untie a filled balloon). This positive pressure is due to the freezing/thawing pattern of spring days in areas like Vermont and Massachusetts. At night, dropping temperatures cause the water within the vessels to freeze: this allows gas to dissolve, thereby compacting the volume and reducing the xylem pressure. At this time, the roots absorb water. During the day, when temperatures increase, xylem sap thaws and releases gas bubbles; this causes the liquid to expand and to create a positive pressure (relative to the atmosphere outside).

Approximately 40 gallons of sap must be collected, boiled, and filtered in order to produce 1 gallon of syrup. Vermont, the largest maple syrup producer in the United States, made 460,000 gallons of maple syrup in 2000, estimated to be worth $13,340,000.

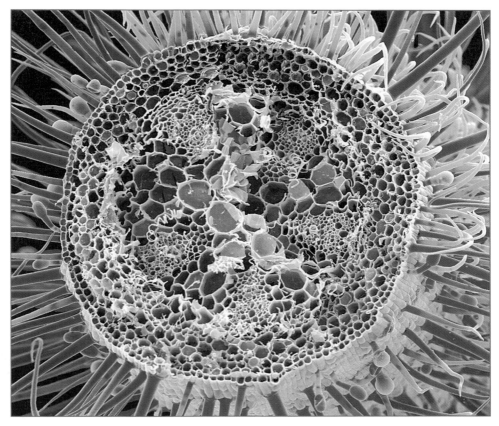

Figure 5.3 Vascular tissues are specialized to transport materials throughout the plant body. The center of this geranium plant stem is filled with large xylem vessels for transporting water and mineral nutrients from the roots to the main body of the plant. Five bundles of phloem tissue (pale green) serve to distribute carbohydrates and other organic molecules around the plant. A ring of parenchyma cells (purple) surrounds the xylem and phloem.

Sieve tube elements undergo an interesting series of developments in order to function as efficient carriers of nutrients when mature. Following cell division, a young cell contains a full set of organelles, but during maturation selective autophagy degrades particular cellular components. The central vacuole, ribosomes, Golgi body, cytoskeleton, and, most notably, the nucleus are all disintegrated. At maturity, all that remains of the protoplast are the plasma membrane, smooth ER, mitochondria, and some plastids. It may be noted that the red blood cells of animals— also transport vehicles—lack a nucleus at maturity. Unlike short-lived blood cells, however, sieve tube elements must remain alive and functional for a long time; this is achieved through a partnership with smaller, neighboring **companion cells.**

Companion cells are specialized parenchyma cells that keep the reduced sieve tube elements alive. They are sister cells of sieve tube elements, a result of unequal cell division from a common mother cell. At maturity, however, companion cells still contain abundant organelles, including a functional nucleus. A companion cell is joined to its respective sieve tube element by numerous cytoplasmic connections, allowing intercellular communication and the passage of much needed materials such as proteins and ATP. Companion cells and sieve tube elements are equally dependent on each other: companion cells keep sieve tube elements alive and when a sieve tube element dies, its associated companion cell dies as well.

Plants do not have a heart to pump phloem sap throughout the plant body; yet, in the absence of such an organ, they are able to move massive amounts of sugar. Movement typically occurs from a **source** (site of photosynthesis) such as a leaf to a **sink** (site of use, either storage or respiration) such as growing tissues or a taproot. The current model that explains this motion, called the **pressure-flow hypothesis,** states that sugar is moved along a sieve tube by a gradient of turgor pressure. Sugar is actively loaded (using energy from ATP) into sieve tubes at its source and actively unloaded into source tissues, creating a concentration gradient within the shared cytoplasm of sieve tube elements. The high concentration of sugar near the source draws in water from neighboring xylem vessels via **osmosis** (the movement of water across a semipermeable membrane), thereby creating pressure. Near the sink tissues, where the concentration of sugar is low, water exits the sieve tube. Thus, the active loading of sugar into the phloem and unloading into source tissues, coupled with osmosis, results in the physical flow of materials from source to sink without the aid of a heart.

The three major tissue systems—dermal, ground, and vascular—have allowed plants to colonize the land. Special cell types and arrangement of these tissues differ markedly between stems, roots, and leaves because of difference in organ functions.

68

Without the flowers, the plant yields no fruit.
Without the emerging fruit, ripeness cannot happen.
— Sri Sathya Sai Baba

Stems

A typical plant consists of two parts: the root system (which is usually belowground) and the shoot system (the majority of which is usually aboveground). The shoot may be further subdivided into two types of organs: a supportive stem and light-capturing leaves. Stems are extremely important organs, as proven by their many functions.

STEM FUNCTIONS

Stems support the aboveground portions of the plant, such as flowers and leaves. Light, which is necessary for photosynthesis in plants, may be a limited commodity in populated, competitive environments. Plants that are growing in dim light, such as underneath the canopy of a forest or a layer of fallen leaves, must elongate to reach the ample light above them. Stem growth and elongation, in various styles, achieve this end by elevating the leaves into better-lit areas.

Stems are important conductive organs. In many plants, the photosynthetic leaves and the water-absorbing roots are separated by great distances and, therefore, must be bridged with vascular tissues. Large trees with massive, wide trunks are an example of how a stem may become devoted to conduction: all but the outer bark is made of vascular tissue.

Stems are also highly effective storage organs for water or food. Desert cacti can persist for long periods of time without rain by storing water reserves in their fleshy, ribbed stems. When a heavy rain actually does drench the desert area, the cactus absorbs large amounts of the rain through its roots and fills its stem like a balloon; the ribbed structure of the stem allows this to occur without it bursting open. Potato **tubers**, among other fleshy, underground stems, are storage organs for starch. Modified stems for food storage allow **perennial** species (plants that live for multiple years) to persist without a photosynthesizing shoot during times of drought or cold. They are also delicious when baked, mashed, or fried!

SHOOT STRUCTURE

Shoot development begins before an **embryo** (young plant within a seed) ever emerges from its seed (Figure 6.1). A seedling's stem is divided into two parts: the **hypocotyl**, which is the embryonic portion below the cotyledons (seed leaves), and the **epicotyl** (the stem above the cotyledons). The epicotyl bears the leaves of a plant at regions known as **nodes**. The regions of stem between two nodes, which may be long or short, are called **internodes** ("between nodes").

Cell division and tissue differentiation of the shoot begins at the shoot tip (**apex**). New cells are added to the shoot in a region called the **shoot apical meristem**, which forms a very tiny dome at the tip. The shoot apical meristem is protected by layers of **leaf primordia**, which are tiny stubs that develop into leaves. As it divides, the shoot apical meristem produces leaf primordia, **bud primordia** (which later grow into lateral branches), and the primary meristems: protoderm, procambium, and ground meristem. The meristematic cells in the apex also regenerate themselves, thus perpetuating the existence of the meristem indefinitely.

Farther down from the meristem of the shoot tip is where the primary meristems differentiate into the dermal, ground, and vascular tissues; this is also where the leaf primordia further develop into leaves. Cell division within an internode is typically uniform throughout its length. In some plants, however, most notably in grasses, internodal division is restricted to a localized region of cells called the **intercalary meristem**. These plants tend to have segmented stems with intercalary meristems situated between two segments; bamboo and corn stalks demonstrate this form of growth.

TISSUE ORGANIZATION IN PRIMARY STEMS

Stems, like roots and leaves, contain each of the three tissue systems: dermal, ground, and vascular. The stems of the **primary**

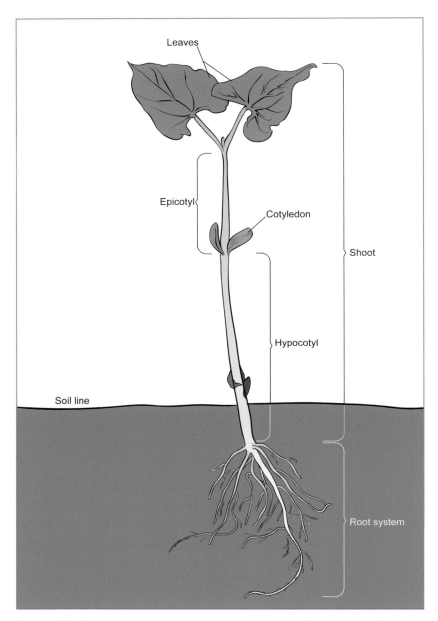

Figure 6.1 The shoot structure of a plant includes its stems and leaves. A seedling's stem is divided into two parts: the hypocotyl, which is the embryonic portion below the cotyledons (seed leaves), and the epicotyl (the stem above the cotyledons).

plant body (no secondary/lateral growth) contain mostly ground tissue. Study of the cell types present, together with the arrangement of the vascular tissue, can be a useful tool for identifying and classifying plants.

The dermal tissue of the primary plant stem typically includes only epidermal cells. The epidermis, which may be one or several cells thick, forms the outermost layer of the stem. A layer of wax, called the cuticle (see Chapter 5), coats the outermost epidermal cells, protecting against water loss to the environment. Specialized epidermal cells of the stem include **guard cells** and **trichomes**, which are discussed in detail in Chapter 8.

Beneath the epidermis is a layer of ground tissue called the **cortex**. Cortex tissue is composed mostly of parenchyma cells, though it may include collenchyma and sclerenchyma as well. Cortical parenchyma cells usually contain photosynthesizing chloroplasts that give stems their familiar green color. Having a photosynthetic stem in addition to photosynthetic leaves increases a plant's productivity by making better use of the sunlight it receives. Cortical collenchyma is found in the stems of some plants: the square stems of alfalfa (*Medicago sativa*), mints (Lamiaceae), and coleus strengthen their corners with bundles of collenchyma. Sclerenchyma cells in the cortex of stems, such as fibers, lend support and rigidity to stems that have stopped elongating.

The central region of a stem, which can make up a significant portion of a stem's volume, is known as the **pith**. Pith tissue often contains only one cell type, parenchyma. Pith parenchyma cells are typically too far inside the stem to receive enough light for photosynthesis. Instead, they perform tasks such as production of biologically important compounds and storage of food and metabolites. The pith also lends support to the stem, which must be able to support a great deal of weight in some cases. Some plants, however, remove their pith's parenchyma cells at maturity, leaving an empty cavity inside of the stem. The vines of pumpkin, squash, and cucumber plants and the stalks of dandelion flowers have very large cavities.

Distribution of conductive tissues varies between different groups of plants. Vascular tissue in the stems of seed plants tends to adopt one of three basic arrangements.

- Gymnosperms and dicotyledonous flowering plants that undergo secondary growth form a cylinder of vascular tissue between the cortex and pith. In this arrangement, xylem is found on the inner part of the cylinder (facing the pith) and phloem occurs toward the outside (facing the cortex).

- **Herbaceous** (nonwoody), dicotyledonous plants tend to organize their vascular tissue in a broken cylinder. The xylem and phloem form a ring of discrete vascular bundles near the periphery of the stem, between the cortex and pith parenchyma. The ground tissue between bundles is composed mostly of parenchyma and is called **interfascicular** parenchyma; it bridges the cortex and the pith.

- Most monocot stems adopt a third arrangement of vascular tissues in which discrete vascular bundles of xylem and phloem are scattered throughout the stem. In such an assembly, the cortex and pith cannot be distinguished from each other and are simply referred to collectively as ground tissue. A cross section of a monocot (corn or *Zea mays*) is shown in Figure 6.2.

SECONDARY GROWTH IN STEMS

Growth by the shoot apex alone would result in tall, skinny plants that would eventually topple over from their own weight. The process of lateral thickening in stems—growth that makes tree trunks get wider each year—is known as **secondary growth**. Secondary thickening of stems occurs through the production of new vascular tissues and a new set of dermal tissues as well.

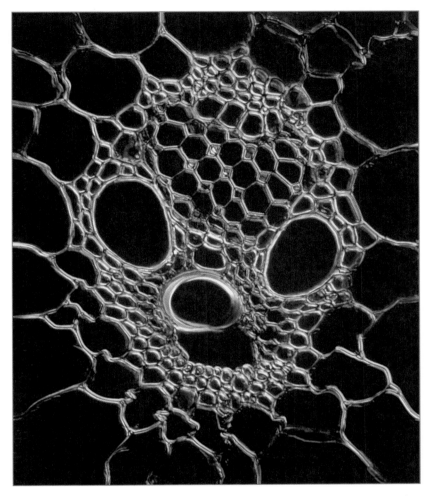

Figure 6.2 A cross-section of a corn stem showing a single vascular bundle. Most monocot stems adopt an arrangement of vascular tissues in which discrete vascular bundles of xylem and phloem are scattered throughout the stem. If this particular vascular bundle were viewed as a person's face, the eyes, forehead, and mouth would correspond to metaxylem vessels, phloem tissue, and a ruptured protoxylem vessel, repectively.

Primary growth at the shoot apex, when coupled with secondary growth in older regions of a plant, leads to vertical and horizontal increases in size (respectively) and makes possible the massive trees that tower in forests throughout the planet. All gymnosperms and many angiosperms undergo secondary growth during their lifetimes, though herbs (nonwoody plants) and monocots do not.

Secondary Production of Vascular Tissue

Secondary vascular tissue in gymnosperms and dicots is produced by the **vascular cambium. Cambium** (plural, cambia) refers to a lateral meristem that produces secondary growth. The vascular cambium, which arises from the procambium during shoot development, is a cylinder of cells that runs along the whole plant stem. Cells that make up the vascular cambium remain undifferentiated and retain their meristematic ability to produce vascular components. The meristematic cells within the vascular bundles of the primary stem are collectively called the **fascicular** cambium. If interfascicular parenchyma separates individual vascular bundles, then the cambium between bundles are called interfascicular cambium. The fascicular and interfascicular cambia together make up the vascular cambium.

Within the vascular cambium are two different meristematic cell types (**initials**): **fusiform initials** and **ray initials**. Fusiform initials, which are elongated and tapered, divide to produce the cells of the vascular tissue (e.g., vessel elements, tracheids, sieve tube elements, and fibers). Ray initials, which have a more cubic shape than fusiform initials, divide to produce radial files of parenchyma cells called **rays.** Rays look like the spokes of a bicycle wheel in a stem cross-section and provide radial transport of water and nutrients between the inside and outside regions of the stem.

Each time that a fusiform initial divides, it produces two different daughter cells: one becomes either xylem or phloem while the other becomes part of the new cambium. This division scheme results in a perpetual maintenance of the vascular cambium throughout many seasons of growth. Daughter cells that become **secondary xylem** (xylem that is produced by the vascular cambium) differentiate to the inside of the stem, while daughter cells that become **secondary phloem** differentiate to the outside of the stem. The result of such growth, when viewed in cross-section, is an outer ring of phloem, an inner ring of xylem, and a layer of vascular cambium between the two. The youngest (most recently differentiated) cells of the two tissues are closest to the cambium, while the older cells are farthest away from the cambium. The result is that old xylem is in the center of the stem and old phloem is near the outside of the stem (Figure 6.3).

Wood, in a botanical sense, is the secondary xylem of a plant. The layers of xylem that accumulate over many years often account for most of the bulk in a woody stem because a given growing season typically produces more xylem than phloem. Temperate woody species that produce secondary xylem create two types of tracheary elements: **spring wood** (or early wood) and **summer wood** (or late wood). The cells of spring wood characteristically have thin walls and large inner diameters to better optimize water conductance to the rapidly expanding buds. In contrast, summer wood cells have thick walls and smaller diameters, though they too transport a great deal of water. The large spring wood and the abutting previous year's summer wood form a boundary that contrasts so discernibly that it creates lines that are visible by the unaided eye. Such lines, which circumnavigate the stem between each year's secondary xylem deposition, are called **growth rings**. Counting the number of growth rings in a stem can accurately reveal the plant's age.

Vascular tissue in older stems eventually ceases to conduct materials. The old xylem in the center of a stem, following its years of service, fills with substances such as oil, gum, resin, and tannin. These compounds plug the tracheary elements, presumably preventing infection yet rendering them unable to conduct; they do, however, continue to support the shoot. The plugged xylem of woody species is called **heartwood**, which is surrounded

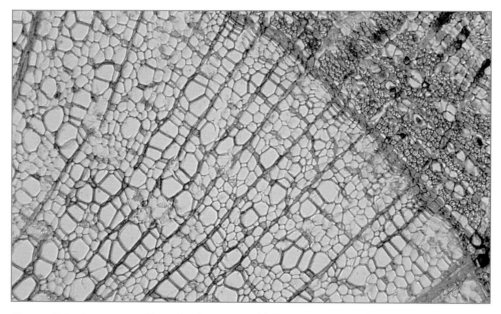

Figure 6.3 A cross-section of a two-year-old lime tree stem shows the second year xylem (bottom left), cambium layer (narrow, green, curved band) and phloem (upper right, striped with pink phloem fibers). Note the rays (dark green lines) of the xylem and phloem.

by the conductive **sapwood** (younger xylem). Heartwood may be darker in color, due to the presence of tannins. Old phloem, unlike xylem, does not have highly lignified cell walls and, thus, is crushed between external dermal tissue and newer phloem. Very old phloem eventually gets sloughed off as bark. As a result, secondary phloem forms a relatively small cylinder when compared to an equivalent year's worth of secondary xylem.

Secondary Production of Dermal Tissues

Increase of stem girth by the vascular cambium alone would rip apart the thin epidermis of the primary plant. Such a situation, therefore, requires a simultaneous production of secondary dermal tissue to replace the inadequate epidermis. To keep pace with the seasonally growing xylem and phloem, which incrementally increase the circumference of the stem, another lateral meristem exists called the **cork cambium**. The cork cambium is a meristematic cylinder of cells that is usually derived from the outer layer of cortex. Unlike the vascular cambium, which contains ray and fusiform initials, cork cambium is made of only one cell type. Furthermore, cork cambium does not regenerate itself indefinitely: after several bouts of cell division, a cork cambium arrests and a new one takes its place. All of the dead tissues to the outside of the youngest cork cambium are collectively known as the **outer bark**. The living tissues from the vascular cambium to the youngest cork cambium—which includes phloem—are known as the **inner bark** of a plant (Figure 6.4).

For a limited time, a particular cork cambium produces two dermal cell types in addition to itself: **cork** and **phelloderm**. The cork, cork cambia, and phelloderm are collectively called the periderm of the stem. Phelloderm cells, which are produced to the inside of the cork cambium, are living parenchyma cells. Cork cells are produced to the outside of the cork cambium and are dead at maturity. They are coated in layers of **suberin** (fatty, waterproof material) and wax, making them impermeable to water and gases; this is to prevent water loss from the stem and infection by outside organisms but makes gas exchange difficult. Oxygen can reach respiring cells within the stem because the periderm contains many pores called **lenticels**, which are regions of spongy tissue containing large spaces between cells to allow gas diffusion. Thus, the epidermis, once the dominant dermal tissue of the primary stem, is soon replaced by periderm in the secondary stem.

MORPHOLOGICAL DIVERSITY OF STEMS

Plant stems come in many shapes and sizes and may be modified to form specialized structures with novel functions. Listed below are just a few of the vast number of stem modifications found in nature.

Figure 6.4 This cross-section of a tree trunk shows the circular band of growth rings, which can be used to determine a tree's age. Each of the growth rings represents a year of growth for the tree. This tree was at least 16 years old.

- Tubers, **corms,** and **rhizomes** are fleshy, underground stems that act as storage organs, often for perennial plants that must last through the winter. Corms, such as those of *Crocus* or *Gladiolus*, are short, upright and covered with papery leaves. Rhizomes (also called root stocks), such as the "root" of ginger, are horizontal stems that are often branched. Tubers, best known from potato plants, are a fleshy type of rhizome with many nodes.

- **Stolons** are long, thin stems that creep along the ground creating roots and new shoots at their nodes/tips. Stolons radiating away from a mother plant may create clones of the original plant as a means of vegetative reproduction. Strawberries are an example of a stolon-bearing plant.

- **Vines** are stems that cannot support themselves alone but instead use other structures or even other plants as a substrate to crawl up. Climbing vines exhibit many varied techniques for gripping their supports, some of which include twining (coiling around, as in morning glory), **tendrils** (peas; see Chapter 8), adhesive appendages (Boston ivy), and barbed roots (English ivy).

- **Thorns** are sharp, modified stems that protect a plant against herbivores and other potentially damaging animals. These woody, reduced branches are born on the main stem axis of many plants, such as hawthorn. Thorns are often confused with prickles and spines, which are modified epidermis and leaves, respectively.

When one tugs at a single thing in nature,
he finds it attached to the rest of the world.
— John Muir

Roots

Following the colonization of land by plants, there became increasing selective pressure on plants to grow taller and in drier environments in response to competition. These pressures eventually favored the evolution of the root. Roots, which typically make up the underground portion of the plant, are complex and important organs. The structure and growth of the root differ from the aboveground shoot (stems and leaves), as do functions between the two systems.

A plant's root is the first structure to emerge from a germinating seed (Figure 7.1). The primary root (first root), which is already formed inside the seed, is called the **radicle**. The radicle breaks through the seed coat and immediately begins to grown downward, regardless of the seed's initial orientation. In gymnosperms and many flowering plants (especially dicots), the primary root persists as the main root axis, continuing to grow down while creating root branches. In this growth habit, the primary root, termed a **taproot**, is larger than the other roots and is capable of growing to extensive depths (Figure 7.2). (According to the *Guinness Book of World Records*, a South African fig tree's roots penetrated a depth of 120 meters or 393.7 feet.[4]) The taproot plus all of its subsidiary roots are collectively called the **taproot system**.

The radicle of monocot plants usually dies shortly after emerging from the germinating seed. Taking over in its place are a number of **adventitious** roots (roots born from shoot tissue, such as the stem) that proliferate and branch. Unlike a taproot system, no single member of this stem-derived root system dominates the others in size, nor is a particular root established as a main axis. Instead, the roots multiply and branch in a netlike fashion, earning the title of a **fibrous root system**. Fibrous root systems are shallower than taproot systems, though they are significantly more extensive.

ROOT FUNCTIONS

The specialized root and shoot systems of a plant complement

Figure 7.1 A plant's root is the first structure to emerge from a germinating seed. The seed coat of this radish seed has split (at top) and a young root has emerged, with root hairs visible.

each other through a division of labor. Aboveground, the green tissues of the shoot photosynthesize, creating sugars that may be used to fuel growth throughout the plant, including the roots.

Figure 7.2 In gymnosperms and many flowering plants (such as the dandelion shown here), the primary root persists as the main root, continuing to grow down while creating root branches. This taproot is larger than the other roots and is capable of growing to extensive depths.

Belowground, the root offers the shoot support and storage. In addition, it provides the shoot water and minerals from the soil, which are essential for growth.

Anchorage and Storage

Roots, by weaving throughout the soil in extensive, fibrous networks or by plunging downward to the depths of the earth with lateral branches, anchor a plant in place to provide support and stability. Tall plants, such as trees, must be able to withstand heavy winds without toppling over; a plant with a deep taproot accomplishes this in the same manner as a telephone pole, which is driven far into the ground to keep it upright. Fibrous roots, on the other hand, grip the soil like thread sewn into cloth: this supports the plant, keeps it in the ground during grazing and prevents erosion of the soil by water.

Plant species that live for more than a year may also employ their roots to act as storage organs. Excess photosynthate from the shoot that is not used for growth can be stored as simple sugars or starch in enlarged, fleshy roots; these reserves allow plants to survive in periods of drought or freezing conditions. Carrots, turnips, sugar beets, and sweet potatoes are examples of taproots that have been modified for storage.

Water and Nutrient Absorption

One of the challenges that a land-dwelling organism faces is acquiring water and minerals from the environment and distributing them throughout its body. Animals that are adapted for life on land may drink water to stay hydrated and consume other organisms for nutrition. A plant must obtain water and minerals in a different way because it is fixed in place and cannot move to water.

Plants absorb almost all of their water through their roots. Beneath the surface of even dry soil is a reservoir of water surrounding the particulate matter (sand, clay, etc.), through which roots grow. In order to be distributed throughout the rest of the plant body, water must penetrate the root surface and reach the vascular tissue within by passing through the **apoplast** (collection of cell walls), the **symplast** (the shared cytoplasm of multiple cells), or both. Water that moves apoplastically traverses freely through the pores and spaces of the cell wall surrounding root protoplasts (apoplast). Water that crosses the plasma membrane of a root cell enters the symplast and may move to adjacent cells via plasmodesmata. Eventually, water must cross at least one membrane and move symplastically before entering the xylem of the plant for distribution.

In addition to water absorption, the roots are also the sole source for nutrient uptake. Soil bacteria produce fixed nitrogen from the atmosphere that is absorbed by roots and used to create amino acids, proteins, DNA, and other organic molecules. Usable nitrogen is often a limited commodity in soils and must be added as fertilizer in most agricultural crops. Roots also acquire many inorganic molecules such as potassium, calcium, chloride, and phosphate from the ground; these are required in small amounts but used in numerous, essential cellular processes. The minerals that are obtained from the soil do not account for much of a plant's mass (water, carbon dioxide, and oxygen dominate the bulk of it), though disease symptoms form if a plant cannot get enough of any particular nutrient.

The highly branched nature of roots, coupled with extensions of epidermal cells, provides the plant with a tremendous amount of subterranean surface area for maximum water uptake. If all of the roots from a 4-month-old rye plant (*Secale cereale*), which are contained in less than 2 cubic feet of soil, were laid end-to-end, they would measure an astounding 387 miles with a surface area of 6,875 square feet![5] As if this weren't enough surface contact with the soil, over 80% of land plants associate with networks of **mycorrhizal fungi** (mycorrhiza means "root fungus"), which significantly increase the absorption area.

ROOT STRUCTURE: FROM THE TIP UP

Root tips continue growing for the entire lifetime of a plant, with the exception of periods of extreme drought or low temperatures. The **root apical meristem** produces cells that differentiate, elongate, and grow while also regenerating and protecting itself. Though such maturation of cell types is a continuous process, there are several distinct zones of a root at any given time. Since tip growth is continuous, it may be useful to think of a longitudinal section of a root as a time-lapse movie of cells dividing, differentiating, and elongating from the tip up.

The fragile meristematic cells of the root apex are protected by a **root cap** that aids in growth through the soil. The root cap is a crown of living parenchyma cells at the root tip that are continuously produced and sloughed off by passing abrasive soil particles. These cells act as fodder during mechanically damaging movement through the ground and actually remain alive in the soil for days following detachment. Such sloughed cells have been proposed to protect the root from the toxic effects of aluminum.[6] Root cap cells produce and secrete a lubricant, called **mucigel**, to facilitate passage through the earth. Perception of gravity, which is essential for effective root growth, also occurs in the root cap cells, most likely through the sediment of amyloplasts (starch granules) within them.

Above the root cap is an area of compact, undifferentiated cells (the root apical meristem) that reside in the **region of cell division**. As the name implies, this zone contains cells that divide frequently to provide the raw material needed for root growth. Root cap cells are generated from this region and are pushed down toward the soil, replenishing the ever-abraded structure. The primary meristems—protoderm, ground meristem, and procambium—are also generated from this region and begin to differentiate into their corresponding tissue systems.

Farther up the root is the highly active **elongation zone**. The elongation zone is the part of the root where the most growth occurs, in terms of increase in length. The walls of cells in this zone loosen, allowing the relatively small protoplasts to swell and expand, thereby elongating the cells and increasing their volume. Expansion of cells in the elongation zone generates the force that pushes the lower root tip farther down and is also responsible for gravitropic movements (bending down toward gravity) in disoriented (sideways; upside-down) roots. Tissues continue to differentiate in this area though specific cell types are already present at this point, namely protoxylem vessel elements.

Above the elongation zone are cells that are no longer expanding; these cells make up the **maturation zone**. In this part of the root, which is now a couple of millimeters from the tip, tissues finish differentiating into their mature form. As they mature, the cells reside in a portion of the root that is no longer subject to the abrasiveness of passing through soil because elongation has ceased. Lateral extensions—**root hairs** and branch roots—form in the mature zone because it is unlikely that they will be sheared off by the soil, as they would be in the regions of elongation and cell division.

ROOT STRUCTURE: CROSS-SECTION OF A MATURE, PRIMARY ROOT

The mature primary root, prior to any secondary growth, is composed of concentric cylinders of the three tissue systems. From the surface to the center, the epidermis forms the outer layer, followed by a middle layer of cortex, and, at the center, the vascular cylinder. This arrangement of tissues effectively absorbs, filters, and transports water from the soil.

A single layer of epidermal cells is the only dermal tissue of the primary root. The root's epidermis, which arises from the protoderm meristem, is the interface between the plant and the soil and facilitates the uptake of water and minerals. To increase water permeability, most root epidermal cells lack a waxy cuticle, enabling water to pass freely into the root from the soil. This is in contrast with the shoot epidermis, which has a waxy cuticle to prevent uncontrolled water loss. Many epidermal cells in the mature root tip (above the elongation zone) have tubular projections called root hairs, so named because, to the naked eye, they look like a tiny fur coat. Root hairs increase the surface area of the root system dramatically with little increase in volume, thus increasing a root's absorbance capability at a small energetic and metabolic cost. As an example, the 4-month-old rye plant mentioned earlier has an estimated 14,335,000,000 root hairs with a combined surface area of 4,321 square feet (401 square meters); that is almost twice the surface area of the rest of the roots! Most of a root's mineral and water absorption occurs at root hairs (Figure 7.3).

Beneath the epidermis is a large region of ground tissue called the **root cortex**. Cortex is often the only ground tissue of the primary root. Some monocots may contain a substantial pith in the root center, though these cells are derived from the procambium and, therefore, are considered to be vascular. The cortex consists of parenchyma cells with nonphotosynthetic plastids such as amyloplasts that function as storage units for starch. Cortex parenchyma usually contains many intercellular spaces that facilitate air and water diffusion to the respiring cells within the root, as well as numerous plasmodesmata connections between adjacent cells to allow symplastic movement of water and nutrients from the soil to the vascular cylinder (Figure 7.4).

The innermost layer of the cortex, called the **endodermis** ("inside skin"), is a special ring of cells designed to prevent apoplastic movement of water into the vascular cylinder. Endodermal cells effectively block movement through the cell walls by forming a waterproof seal of suberin wax around four of their six cell walls. Such a seal is called the **Casparian strip** because, when viewed under a microscope in cross-section, it looks like a band. The Casparian strip surrounds the vascular cylinder and forces water to cross at least one plasma membrane before entering the xylem. By requiring symplastic movement of water, the plant

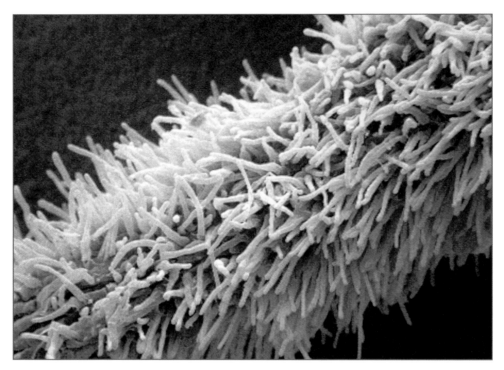

Figure 7.3 Root hairs increase the surface area of the root system with little increase in volume. Most of a root's mineral and water absorption occurs at root hairs. Shown here is a root of marjoram (magnified 100x).

gains control over its rate of water uptake. Symplastic transport also serves to filter the water and nutrients before distributing them to the rest of the plant. As they age, endodermal cells eventually coat their remaining walls with suberin and wax, thereby leaving plasmodesmata as the only passageway into the vascular cylinder. Some cells, called **passage cells**, persist with only their Casparian strip as the waterproof barrier and become the chief water-conducting cells of the endodermis.

The vascular cylinder (**stele**) is derived from the meristematic procambium and is in the center of the root. Its outermost layer, which lies in contact with the inside face of the endodermis, is a ring of cells called the **pericycle**. The pericycle is a layer of

Figure 7.4 Water that is absorbed from the soil must pass through several tissues before reaching the xylem (center). Once past the epidermis on the root surface, water and minerals must penetrate the thick cortex, restrictive endodermic, and pericycle before they can be transported to the rest of the plant body by vessels. Two (of four) groups of phloem cells are shown in the center, between the xylem and poles.

parenchyma cells that are important in generating lateral roots as well as lateral cambia needed for secondary growth. These parenchyma cells may or may not become lignified for additional strength. The pericycle encircles the two vascular tissues: xylem and phloem.

Xylem, in the absence of pith, forms the center of the vascular cylinder and, therefore, the center of the root in eudicots. Maturation of primary root xylem occurs from the outside to the inside so that the xylem on the outside is protoxylem (because it differentiated during cell elongation) and the central xylem is metaxylem (because it differentiated and matured after elongation had finished taking place). The protoxylem that differentiated during root elongation forms ridges of outer xylem, like the ridges of a Phillips screwdriver. Protoxylem ridges, when viewed in cross-section, appear to extend out from the metaxylem to the pericycle (specifically to passage cells, from which they receive water); in this view, they are referred to as **protoxylem poles**. The number of protoxylem poles/ridges varies between plant species and even within a single plant: a root with two poles is called a **diarch** root; three poles is a **triarch** root; four poles is a **tetrarch** root; more than four poles earns the title of a **polyarch** root. Phloem tissue in roots occurs in strands between the xylem ridges. The number of phloem strands equals the number of protoxylem poles.

SECONDARY GROWTH IN ROOTS

Monocots do not typically exhibit secondary growth of their shoots or roots. In the case of many dicots, however, especially woody dicots, the belowground root system must thicken along with the aboveground shoot for anchorage purposes. Imagine what would happen if a 200-year-old oak tree had only slender primary roots to keep it standing upright.

The vascular cambium in roots is derived from procambial cells between the primary vascular tissues as well as pericycle cells. The cells between the xylem and phloem, which retain their meristematic capabilities, form multiple individual vascular cambia whose numbers depend on the number of phloem strands. These cambia immediately divide to form secondary xylem, thus pushing the phloem strands outward. Meanwhile, the pericycle generates vascular cambia at the protoxylem poles such that a continuous ring of vascular cambium surrounds the xylem with primary phloem to the outside. Subsequent divisions of the vascular cambium resemble that in the stem, adding layers of new secondary xylem (wood) to the inside and new secondary phloem to the outside.

Unlike the first cork cambium of stems, which usually arises from ground tissue, root cork cambia arise from the pericycle of the vascular cylinder. As a result, all of the tissues to the outside of the pericycle (i.e., endodermis, cortex, and epidermis) are sloughed off and replaced by peridermal tissue in roots with secondary growth. The periderm of roots is similar to that in stems: it is composed of cork cambia, cork, and phelloderm. Root periderm also contains lenticels for gas exchange, allowing oxygen to diffuse into the intercellular spaces from the soil.

8 Leaves

*Birth, life, and death—each took place
on the hidden side of a leaf.*

— Toni Morrison

Leaves

Leaves are specialized organs that perform the majority of photosynthesis in plants. The stem elevates leaves from the ground such that they may better absorb sunlight, the energy used to build sugars from atmospheric carbon dioxide.

LEAF FUNCTIONS

A true leaf is a highly advanced structure whose primary function is to perform photosynthesis, though some leaves are modified for additional or alternative tasks. Generally speaking, a leaf's form reflects its ability to capture sunlight, exchange gases, and compete with other plants.

Leaves produce almost all of a plant's sugars through photosynthesis. Like solar panels, leaves have relatively large surface areas to capture sunlight. The light that falls upon leaves is absorbed by chloroplast-rich ground tissue, and the energy is used to drive the photosynthetic reactions. Leaves are also perforated with tiny pores that allow air to diffuse into intercellular airspaces, providing the chloroplasts with a supply of carbon dioxide, which is the raw material that is used to build sugar molecules. Leaves, with the energy, materials, and biochemical machinery needed for photosynthesis, can be thought of as green sugar factories.

Leaves are important players in the transport of water. Water is absorbed from the soil by the root system and loaded into the xylem. A continuous column of water molecules extends up through the vessels of the stem where they eventually reach the ground tissues of the leaf. Water evaporates off of the surface of these ground tissue cells and becomes vapor within the intercellular airspaces of the leaf interior. As they change from liquid to gas, water molecules pull the entire column of water up through the stem so that the next layer of molecules wet the surface and can evaporate. The water vapor then exits the leaf through the same pores that carbon dioxide enters and is incorporated into the outside atmosphere. This process of water loss, including both the evaporation of liquid water into a gas and diffusion of gaseous water out the leaf, is known as **transpiration**. Transpiration accounts for more than 90% of the water lost by plants and is necessary for moving large amounts of water up to the tops of tall plants and trees; the positive pressure generated by the roots would not be able to push water much higher than a few feet.

Beyond photosynthesis and transpiration, leaves may have other functions as well. Some leaves become extremely broad to absorb as much sunlight as possible, leaving little light for other plants growing below. This greedy light gathering is a form of competition with other plants where light may be a limiting resource. Other leaves are very thick and fleshy. These swollen, or **succulent,** leaves may store water in dry environments, as is true of aloe and jade plants, or starches, as is seen in the underground, non-green leaves of onion bulbs.

LEAF MORPHOLOGY

The forms and shapes of leaves are varied and diverse. A particular plant species' leaves often reflects the environment in which it inhabits: a lily pad leaf is broad and spongy so that it may float on water, while a desert agave has swollen, leathery, and sharp leaves to protect against water loss and thirsty animals.

Most dicotyledonous leaves have a thin, flattened portion called a **blade** (or lamina) that attaches to the stem by means of a **petiole** (leaf stalk, such as the edible part of celery or rhubarb). The expanded blade is the chief photosynthetic part of the leaf, while the petiole extends the blade away from the stem. Some leaves connect directly to the stem without a petiole; leaves such as these are said to be **sessile**. Most monocot plants, especially grasses such as corn, have sessile leaves whose bases wrap around the stem; a leaf base that surrounds the stem is called a **sheath**. Some plants, such as roses, have pairs of leaf-like appendages at the petiole-stem junction called **stipules**. Stipules may function to protect young, growing leaves or act as photosynthetic blades, as in pea plants.

Leaves may be either **simple** or **compound**. If a leaf blade is entire (not divided), then it is called a simple leaf. If the leaf blade, however, is divided into two or more **leaflets** then it is called compound. A compound leaf may bear all of its leaflets on the same point on the petiole; such a leaf is said to be **palmately compound.** Some compound leaves bear their leaflets along a central stalk called a **rachis;** these leaves are **pinnately compound.** Sometimes it is difficult to tell whether one is looking at a simple leaf or the leaflet of a compound leaf. A leaf, by definition, has an **axillary bud** that can develop into a lateral branch. Axillary buds are located in the joint between the stem and the leaf; the most famous of these are brussel sprouts, the enlarged axillary buds of *Brassica oleracea.* Leaflets do not have axillary buds where they join the rachis, thus the presence or absence of an axillary bud is a useful key in determining whether a leaf is compound or simple.

Phyllotaxy, which is the arrangement of leaves along a stem, varies between species or sometimes within an individual plant, but the variations fall into three categories and can be useful for identification purposes. **Alternate** leaf arrangement describes nodes that bear one leaf each. **Opposite** leaf arrangement refers to two leaves that are born at a single node, often 180° apart. Plants that have three or more leaves at each node are said to have a **whorled** leaf arrangement.

LEAF STRUCTURE

The leaf, like the stem and the root, is composed of dermal tissue, ground tissue, and vascular tissue. The three tissues function in concert to efficiently produce and transport sugars for the rest of the plant.

Dermal Tissue

The epidermis covers the lower and upper surfaces of a leaf, protecting it from damage and water loss. Leaves do not undergo secondary growth as roots and stems do, thus the epidermis remains the only dermal tissue in these organs. Like the epidermal cells of the stem, these tightly arranged cells have a waxy coat (cuticle) that helps prevent water from evaporating through the surface of the leaf in an uncontrolled manner. Some plants that inhabit very dry environments may have several layers of epidermal cells as an added measure to retain water. Epidermal cells typically lack chloroplasts and may sometimes have interlocking, puzzle-piece shapes.

Trichomes, commonly referred to as leaf hairs, are specialized structures that form on the surface of leaf epidermises. Unlike root hairs, which are tubular extensions of epidermal cells, trichomes are specialized structures that are distinct from the bulk of the epidermis. A variety of trichomes have been described, ranging from unicellular to multicellular projections, either of which may be filamentous, slightly branched, highly branched, or **glandular** (able to secrete a chemical or substance). The function of leaf hairs varies with the structure, but the following list encapsulates some of the more noteworthy roles.

Protection: Trichomes limit access of insects to the surface of the leaf. Special hooked trichomes have been observed to impale adult insects and their larvae, killing them before they can do substantial damage. Other trichomes contain poisonous chemicals or hallucinogens, such as the resin glands of marijuana (*Cannabis sativa*).

Sunscreen: A dense coat of trichomes helps to reflect some of the solar radiation that bombards plants in sunny areas. This helps keep the plants cool.

Water retention: Hairy leaves help reduce the amount of water lost through transpiration. By trapping moisture at the surface of the leaf, trichomes create a locally humid environment in much the same way that a wool sweater prevents sweat from evaporating off of a person on a hot day.

Carnivory: The inner surface of a Venus flytrap (*Dionea*) has sensitive trichomes that trigger the closing of the trap when stimulated by movement. Glandular trichomes then secrete enzymes and acids to digest the prey for nourishment.

Stinging Nettle Trichomes

Anyone who has ever accidentally touched a stinging nettle (*Urtica dioica*) knows how powerful a leaf hair can be. The leaves and stems of nettles are covered with needle-like trichomes that deliver a painful sting and leave a person's skin with red, painful, persistent welts. Stinging hairs are highly effective protective structures and have been described in at least four plant families.

The hairs of *U. dioica* are shaped like elongated teardrops. At the base of each trichome is a large, multicellular bulb that is embedded in the epidermal cells and that produces the pain-inducing chemicals. The long, narrow shaft that extends from the bulb protrudes approximately 1 millimeter (.1 centimeter) from the plant surface and is capped by a fragile, bulbous tip. The cell walls of these epidermal emergences have silica depositions that make them extremely brittle. When touched, the fragile tip breaks off, leaving the narrow shaft exposed like a glass hypodermic needle. The shaft is sufficient to puncture an animal's skin and deliver the stinging (urticating) intracellular fluid.

Prior to the late 1880s, it was presumed that the stinging substance in nettles was formic acid, which accounts for the painful sting of some ant bites. Biochemical analysis, however, has identified several urticating substances that include acetylcholine and seratonin (both neurotransmitters) as well as leukotrienes and histamines (both potent allergens). These chemicals, in addition to others, constitute the ingredients of a painful cocktail, which effectively delivers immediate, lasting pain and inflammation to any unlucky animal that comes in contact with the plant.

The leaf epidermis is perforated with hundreds of thousands of pores called **stomata** (singular, **stoma**, which is Greek for "mouth"). Stomata permit atmospheric carbon dioxide to enter the leaf in order to be fixed by photosynthesis; they also control transpiration by regulating how much water vapor may escape into the atmosphere from the intercellular spaces of the leaf. Some leaves have their stomata restricted to either the upper or lower side, while others have them present on both; it makes sense, for instance, that water lily leaves have no stomata on the undersides. The leaves of some drought-adapted plants have their stomata sunken into trichome-rich cavities that reduce transpiration by trapping humidity while allowing carbon dioxide to diffuse readily.

It is necessary for the plant to regulate its stomata because of their dual role in water loss and carbon dioxide uptake. If stomata were always open, sugar synthesis could go on continuously throughout the day, but the plant would likely lose too much water and die. Conversely, if stomata were always closed, water would be retained yet not enough sugars could be produced for the plant to stay alive. Many environmental factors such as light, temperature, time of day/night, and the concentration of carbon dioxide influence whether or not stomata are open. Stresses, such as drought, also affect the stomata.

A stoma includes two tubular, chloroplast-containing guard cells that surround and control the **aperture** (opening) of the pore such that it may be opened and closed. The cell walls of guard cells are thickened by radial cellulose microfibrils that restrict lateral expansion while allowing expansion along the length. Furthermore, the guard cells of a particular stoma are joined at the tips such that the ends of the guard cells remain at a relatively fixed distance from each other. When the protoplasts of guard cells swell with water, then the stomata open. When water leaves the guard cells, the stomata close. At first, this may seem backward, but the physical constraints placed on the guard cells in conjunction with protoplast swelling cause them to bow and, therefore, increase the pore between them (Figure 8.1).

Ground Tissue

Almost all of the photosynthesis that occurs in a leaf takes place within the **mesophyll** cells, which account for most of the leaf ground tissue. Mesophyll, which literally means "middle of the leaf," is composed of parenchyma cells with many chloroplasts. Two types of mesophyll cells exist, **palisade parenchyma** and **spongy parenchyma**. Palisade parenchyma consists of long, narrow cells that are oriented in an upright manner such that they look like a fence (palisade means "fence"). The densely packed palisade parenchyma cells effectively absorb sunlight as it passes through the leaf. Spongy parenchyma cells are irregularly shaped and are surrounded by numerous intercellular airspaces, giving the tissue its spongy appearance. The airspaces surrounding the spongy mesophyll are important for circulating carbon dioxide to the photosynthesizing cells. Palisade parenchyma is located above the spongy parenchyma in many leaves, though certain species have a layer of palisade parenchyma sandwiching the spongy parenchyma (Figure 8.2). Some leaves, such as those of corn, do not have distinguishable palisade parenchyma.

Parenchyma cells that surround the vascular bundles (veins) of the leaf form a layer known as the **bundle sheath**. Bundle sheath cells are intermediates between the conductive vascular tissues and the photosynthetic mesophyll cells, playing a major role in material exchange. In this respect, the bundle sheaths of leaves are analogous to the endodermis of the root. Some plants of hot and dry environments, called **C$_4$ plants** because their first photosynthetic product is a four-carbon molecule, restrict their sugar synthesis to the bundle sheath cells alone. Isolating sugar production to the bundle sheath cells increases the plant's photosynthetic efficiency and helps to reduce water loss: reducing the requirement for CO_2 means that the stomata need not

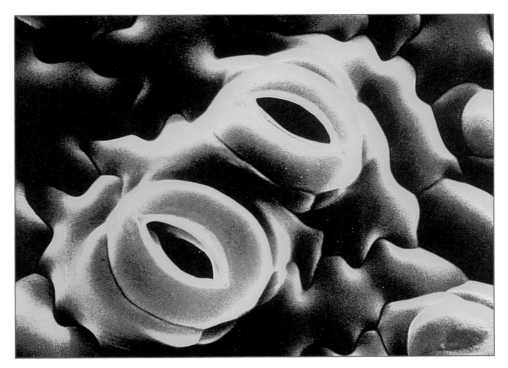

Figure 8.1 The leaf epidermis is perforated with hundreds of thousands of pores called stomata. A stoma includes two tubular, chloroplast-containing guard cells that surround and control the opening of the pore so that it may be opened and closed. When the protoplasts of guard cells swell with water, then the stomata open. When water leaves the guard cells, the stomata close. An electron scanning micrograph of open stomata on the surface of a tobacco leaf is shown here (magnified 450x).

be open as much. C_4 grasses, such as corn, wreath their vascular bundles with an inner bundle sheath and an outer layer of mesophyll, an arrangement called **Kranz anatomy** (*Kranz* is German for "wreath"). **C_3 plants**, such as wheat, have bundle sheaths but do not have Kranz anatomy.

Leaves may also contain a significant amount of collenchyma and sclerenchyma. The petioles of rhubarb and celery, as previously mentioned, contain strands of collenchyma that lend additional support to the leaves. Some species, especially certain monocotyledons, also have strong fibers in their leaves that are

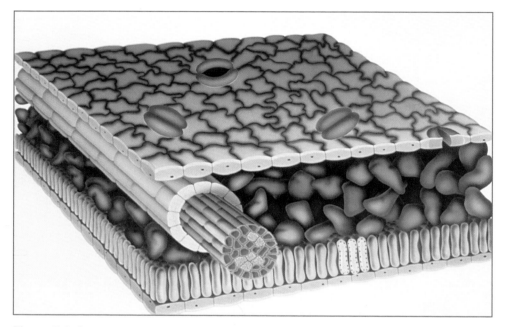

Figure 8.2 Leaves are specialized organs for photosynthesis. The leaf underside (top) has many stomata (brown) within the epidermis to exchange gases between the leaf interior and the atmosphere. Mesophyll cells, consisting of chloroplast-rich spongy parenchyma (green) and palisade parenchyma (yellow) perform most of the plant's photosynthetic reactions. At center left, a leaf vein (vascular bundle) is surrounded by a bundle sheath (orange); within the sheath are xylem (pink) and phloem (white) cells.

cultivated and used for economic products. Sclereids may also be found within a leaf; supportive sclereids, for example, are found in the leaves of water lilies.

Vascular Tissues

Veins, which are bundles of vascular tissue, are embedded throughout the mesophyll of a leaf. The arrangement of veins throughout a leaf, or **venation**, differs among plants. Leaves of dicotyledonous plants typically have a **netted venation** pattern in which the veins branch and intersect regularly. Monocotyledonous plants tend to have **parallel venation** in which the veins extend side-by-side along the length of the leaves. The veins of both arrangement types extend throughout the leaf such that any particular mesophyll cell is no more than a couple cells' distance from a vein (Figure 8.3). The xylem and phloem of veins are continuous with the vascular tissues of the stem and root.

Veins of different sizes may be found within a leaf. The largest, **major veins** carry large quantities of sap to their destinations. The most notable major vein runs down the center of the leaf and is called the **midrib**. Smaller **minor veins** branch from the major veins and are largely responsible for material exchange (water, sugars) with the mesophyll. In this sense, it is appropriate to draw a comparison between the circulatory system of animals and the venation of plants. Large arteries and major veins are chiefly involved in massive transport of fluids (blood and sap, respectively), while the smaller capillaries and minor veins are the sites of exchange with the surrounding tissues.

Xylem tissue occupies the upper portion of a leaf vein and delivers water to the mesophyll and epidermal cells. In addition to hydrating the leaf cells, this water is important for moistening the surfaces of photosynthesizing mesophyll cells. Moist surfaces of the palisade and spongy parenchyma is important because carbon dioxide must dissolve in water before it may cross the plasma membrane and enter the chloroplasts. The wet mesophyll surfaces are also the site of water evaporation, the process that drives water up the stem during transpiration.

Phloem tissue occupies the lower portion of leaf veins. Initially the phloem brings sugars to young, expanding leaves that have high energy requirements from other parts of the plant (e.g., storage cells in the root). Later, in mature leaves that are no longer using energy to grow, the phloem exports the products of photosynthesis out to the rest of the plant.

MORPHOLOGICAL DIVERSITY OF LEAVES

Plant leaves, as photosynthetic apparatuses, display a tremendous variety of shapes and sizes but may be further modified for

Figure 8.3 **A.** Monocotyledonous plants tend to have parallel venation in which the major veins extend side-by-side along the length of the leaves. **B.** Leaves of dicotyledonous plants typically have a netted venation pattern in which the veins branch and intersect regularly.

additional or alternate functions. Listed below are some examples of modified leaves whose primary functions are not photosynthesis.

- Tendrils are small, twining organs that are used to climb up existing structures. Many garden plants including cucumbers, peas, and beans have tendrils that help support their shoot systems. Tendrils can detect when they have come in contact with something and respond by rapidly coiling around it many times, thereby grasping the structure and pulling the plant toward it.

- **Spines** are modified leaves or stipules that protect the plant from herbivory, like the stem-derived thorns described in Chapter 6. Spines are hard, nonphotosynthetic structures.

- **Carnivorous traps** are leaves that have been specialized for extracting nitrogen from insects in regions with nutrient-poor growing conditions (e.g., bogs). The well-known Venus flytrap (*Dionea*) forms hinged traps that rapidly close on its prey. Sundew plants (*Drosera*) have flypaper-like leaves that are covered in sticky hairs and that coil around captive insects. Several carnivorous plants, such as *Nepenthes* and *Sarracenia*, create fluid-filled pitchers with their leaves; insects fall into these pitchers by the dozens, drown, and are digested for nutrients.

- **Flowers**, the reproductive structures in angiosperms, are made of several types of modified leaves. The sepals, petals, stamens, and carpels are each special types of leaves that have been altered for sexual purposes.

Notes

1. A. E. Porsild, C. R. Harington, and G. A. Mulligan, "*Lupinus arcticus* Wats. Grown from Seeds of Pleistocene Age." *Science* 158 (1967): 113–14.

2. Brian E. S. Gunning, and Martin W. Steer, *Ultrastructure and the Biology of Plant Cells* (London: Edward Arnold, 1975).

3. U.S. Department of the Treasury. "Frequently Asked Questions: Currency," Accessed on 1/4/06 http://www.treas.gov/education/faq/currency/production.shtml.

4. Deepest Root. Accessed on 1/4/06 http://www.guinnessworldrecords.com.

5. Howard J. Dittmer, "A Quantitative Study of the Roots and Root Hairs of a Winter Rye Plant (*Secale Cereale*)." *American Journal of Botany* 24, no. 7 (1937): 417–20.

6. Jian-Wei Pan, Dan Ye, Li-Ling Wang, et al, "Root Border Cell Development Is a Temperature-Insensitive and Al-Sensitive Process in Barley." *Plant Cell Physiology* 45, no. 6 (2004): 751–60.

Actin—Protein subunits that make up microfilaments.

Adenine—A nitrogenous base in DNA and RNA.

Adventitious—Originating from an unusual place, such as roots originating from the stem.

Alternate—Leaf arrangement in which there is only one leaf per node.

Amino acids—The molecular building blocks of polypeptides/proteins.

Amyloplast—A starch-filled, colorless plastid.

Anaphase—The third stage of mitosis, in which sister chromatids are separated to opposite ends of the cell.

Angiosperm—A flowering plant.

Annular—In the form of a ring.

Anticodon—Three consecutive nitrogenous bases on a tRNA molecule that are complementary to a codon of mRNA.

Aperture—Opening or pore, as in a stoma.

Apex—Tip, as in the shoot or root.

Apoplast—The shared cell walls of a plant or organ.

Archaea—Single-celled, prokaryotic organisms that live in extreme environments.

Aster—A microtubule organizing center plus its spindle fibers.

ATP (adenosine triphosphate)—The molecule that acts as the energy currency of the cell.

Autophagy—A process in which whole organelles are digested by the vacuole.

Axillary bud—An undeveloped lateral branch located in the joint between the stem and the leaf.

Base pair—The pair of nitrogenous bases that connects the complementary strands of DNA or double-stranded RNA.

Blade—The broad, often thin portion of a leaf.

Bordered pits—Interruptions of the secondary cell wall in tracheids, through which water must pass.

Glossary

Bud primordia—Tiny outgrowths produced by the shoot apical meristem that will eventually become lateral shoots.

Bundle sheath—Layer(s) of cells surrounding a vein.

C_3 plant—A plant whose first photosynthetic product is a 3-carbon molecule.

C_4 plant—A plant whose first photosynthetic product is a 4-carbon molecule.

Cambium—A lateral meristem that produces secondary growth.

Carnivorous trap—A modified leaf that attracts, captures, and kills animals from which it extracts nutrients.

Carotene—An orange carotenoid, as in carrot roots.

Carotenoid—Class of accessory pigments in chloroplasts and chromoplasts that look orange, yellow, or red.

Casparian strip—A band of waterproof primary cell wall that surrounds cells of the root endodermis.

Cell—The basic unit of life. In plants, this consists of a protoplast and its cell wall.

Cell cycle—The sequence of events that occur during division of one cell into two.

Cell division—Process by which two cells are formed from a single precursor.

Cell enlargement—Increase in cell volume by protoplast swelling and cell wall loosening.

Cell plate—A sheet of membrane-bound cell wall materials that expands during cytokinesis to form the middle lamella that separates the resulting daughter cells.

Cell sap—The fluid within the vacuole.

Cellulose—The primary component of plant cell walls.

Cell wall—The highly complex external covering of plant cells that is made primarily of cellulose.

Centromere—A region of chromosome where sister chromatids and kinetochores attach.

Chlorophyll—Light-absorbing molecule of chloroplasts that gives plants their green color.

Chloroplast—A plastid that performs photosynthesis.

Chromatin—DNA that is bound to proteins.

Chromoplast—A colored plastid, as found in flowers and fruits.

Chromosome—A condensed molecule of DNA that contains hereditary information. Following DNA replication, chromosomes consist of two identical sister chromatids that are joined together by a centromere.

Cisterna—Flattened sacs, as in the endoplasmic reticulum or Golgi body.

Codon—Three consecutive nitrogenous bases on mRNA that correspond to a particular amino acid.

Collenchyma—A flexible ground-tissue type composed of irregularly shaped cells with thick primary cell walls.

Companion cell—A phloem cell that associates with a sieve tube element in angiosperms.

Complementary—Describes two strands of either DNA or RNA whose sequences will bind to one another, with guanine (G) binding to cytosine (C) and adenine (A) binding to either thymine (T) or uracil (U).

Compound—Describes a leaf whose blade is divided into leaflets.

Cork—A waterproof dermal tissue of some stems that is produced through secondary growth via the cork cambium.

Cork cambium—A lateral meristem that produces periderm.

Corm—An underground stem that has been modified for storage, as in *Crocus*.

Cortex—Ground tissue between the epidermis and the vascular tissues, as in roots and stems.

Cotyledon—Seed leaf; embryonic structure that provides food for the dormant embryo and germinating seedling.

Crista—The highly folded inner membranes of mitochondria.

Crossing over—Process by which homologous chromosomes physically swap segments of DNA with one another; contributes to genetic variation through sexual reproduction.

Glossary

Cuticle—Waterproof layer that coats epidermal cells in the shoot.

Cytokinesis—Division of cytoplasm of a cell following mitosis or meiosis. In plants, this involves synthesis of a new cell wall.

Cytoplasm—The cytosol and all of its contents, excluding the nucleus.

Cytoskeleton—A flexible framework within the cell made of microtubules and microfilaments.

Cytosine—A nitrogenous base in DNA and RNA.

Cytosol—The solution within the plasma membrane, within which the organelles and cytoskeleton are suspended.

Daughter nucleus—One of two newly formed nuclei following mitosis or meiosis.

Degrade—Disassembly into core units, as in microtubules into tubulin.

Dermal tissue system—The outermost layer(s) of the plant body; epidermis or periderm.

Desmotubule—A strand of endoplasmic reticulum that passes through a plasmodesma and is shared between two adjacent cells.

Diarch—A root with two protoxylem poles.

Dicotyledon (dicot)—A member of the flowering plant class Dicotyledonae, whose plants have two cotyledons (seed leaves). Dicots typically have taproots, netted venation, and floral parts in fours and fives.

Differentiation—The process by which cells develop distinct structural or biochemical properties.

DNA (deoxyribonucleic acid)—An inherited molecule that contains information for a cell's proteins.

Elongation zone—The region near the root tip where the most length increase occurs.

Embryo—A young plant within a seed.

Endodermis—The innermost layer of cortex cells, which surrounds the vascular cylinder in roots.

Endoplasmic reticulum—A network of membranous sacs or tubes.

Envelope—A double membrane, as in plastids and nuclei.

Epicotyl—A portion of the stem that occurs above the cotyledons.

Epidermis—A protective dermal tissue that surrounds the primary plant body.

ER lumen—Fluid-filled cavity within the endoplasmic reticulum.

Eukaryote—An organism with a nucleus and membranous organelles within its cell(s). Animals, fungi, plants, and protists are eukaryotes.

Fiber—A long, narrow sclerenchyma cell.

Fibrous root system—Highly branched roots of roughly equivalent size in which there is no main axis.

Flowers—Reproductive structure in angiosperms that consists of several types of modified leaves.

Fusiform initial—Meristematic cell of the vascular cambium that divides to produce longitudinal cells of the vascular tissue (e.g., vessel elements or sieve tube elements).

G_1 checkpoint—Control mechanism that allows or restricts progression from the G_1 phase to the S phase.

G_1 phase—Period of interphase characterized by intense activity and growth.

G_2 checkpoint—Control mechanism that allows or restricts progression from the G_2 phase into mitosis.

G_2 phase—Final stage of interphase in which final preparations for cell division are made.

Gamete—A cell or nucleus that fuses sexually to form a zygote.

Gene—A section of DNA that contains information for a single polypeptide or RNA molecule.

Glandular—A structure, such as certain trichomes, that secretes a substance.

Glycogen—A branched polysaccharide similar to starch that is used for food storage in animals.

Golgi body—A group of flattened, disk-shaped, membranous sacs that sort and process proteins or secreted material.

Glossary

Grana—Stacks of thylakoid membranes, found in actively photosynthesizing chloroplasts.

Ground meristem—Primary meristem that produces ground tissues.

Ground tissue system—Parenchyma, collenchyma, and sclerenchyma that accounts for the bulk of most plants.

Growth—An increase in volume, usually through a combination of cell division and enlargement.

Growth rings—Boundaries between successive years' secondary xylem.

Guanine—A nitrogenous base in DNA and RNA.

Guard cells—Paired epidermal cells in the shoot that control gas exchange via stomata by opening or closing the pore.

Gymnosperm—A nonflowering seed plant, such as a conifer.

Heartwood—Older, nonconducting xylem in the center of some tree trunks.

Helical—Spiral, like a spring.

Hemicellulose—Cell wall materials that link cellulose microfibrils together.

Herbaceous—Nonwoody.

Herbivore—An animal that eats plants.

Homologous chromosomes—Condensed DNA molecules of comparable size and shape with similar hereditary information (genes).

Hydrophilic—A molecule that is attracted to water.

Hydrophobic—A molecule that is repelled by water.

Hypocotyl—A portion of a seedling's stem, below the cotyledons.

Indeterminate growth—Unlimited growth, as in the apical meristems.

Initial—Meristematic cell within the vascular cambium, of which there are two types—fusiform and ray.

Inner bark—In plants that have undergone secondary growth, the living tissues from the vascular cambium to the youngest cork cambium; includes phloem.

Intercalary meristem—Self-perpetuating region of undifferentiated cells at the nodes of the shoot, from which new cells arise, as in bamboo.

Interfascicular—Between the vascular bundles.

Internode—Region of the stem between two nodes.

Interphase—The period of cell cycle between mitosis or meiosis, during which growth occurs.

Kinetochore—A protein complex that bridges the centromeres of chromosomes to spindle fibers of the mitotic spindle.

Kinetochore microtubule—A spindle fiber that is attached to a centromere by a protein complex.

Kranz anatomy—Wreath-like arrangement of mesophyll and bundle-sheath cells around vascular bundles of leaves (typical of C_4 plants).

Leaflet—A single-blade unit of a compound leaf.

Leaf primordia—Tiny outgrowths produced by the shoot apical meristem that will eventually become leaves.

Lenticel—A region of spongy tissue within the periderm that allows gas exchange to occur between the stem and the atmosphere.

Leucoplast—A colorless plastid.

Lignin—A complex molecule that confers strength to cell walls, as in wood.

Lipid—A class of molecules that do not dissolve in water and include fats and oils.

Lipid bilayer—Two layers of lipids stacked together with their hydrophobic tails together.

Lysosome—A membrane-bound organelle in eukaryotes whose function is to digest large molecules.

Major vein—A large bundle of xylem and phloem in a leaf whose function is primarily that of transport.

Maturation zone—The oldest portion of the root in which cells have finished elongating; demarcated by the presence of root hairs.

Meiosis—The process by which four genetically distinct cells are produced, each with reduced chromosome content.

Glossary

Membrane-bound vesicle—A small, fluid-filled body surrounded by a single lipid bilayer.

Meristem—A self-perpetuating region of undifferentiated cells from which new cells arise.

Mesophyll—Photosynthetic ground tissue of leaves.

Messenger RNA (mRNA)—A complementary copy of a gene that carries information from the nucleus to the ribosome for protein synthesis.

Metabolite—A molecule that is necessary for life (e.g., sugars, amino acids).

Metaphase—The second stage of mitosis, in which chromosomes are aligned along the division plane of the cell.

Metaxylem—Xylem cells that differentiate in a region that is no longer elongating.

Microfibril—A strong cable of many cellulose molecules twisted together.

Microfilament—A long filament that is part of the cytoskeleton.

Microtubule—A long, narrow tube that is part of the cytoskeleton.

Microtubule organizing center—A pole at one end of a dividing cell where spindle fibers converge.

Middle lamella—The layer between two adjacent cells.

Midrib—The largest major vein that runs down the center of the leaf.

Minor vein—A small bundle of xylem and phloem in the leaf whose function is primarily that of material exchange.

Mitochondria—Bacteria-like organelles that create energy for the cell via respiration.

Mitochondrial matrix—The fluid within the inner membrane of the mitochondria.

Mitosis—The process by which duplicated chromosomes separate to form two identical daughter nuclei.

Mitotic spindle—An array of bundled microtubules that forms at each end of a dividing cell.

Molecular motor—A protein that uses energy to move along the cytoskeleton.

Monocotyledon (monocot)—A member of the flowering plant class Monocotyledonae, whose plants have one cotyledon (seed leaf). Monocots typically have fibrous roots, parallel venation, and floral parts in threes.

Mucigel—A slimy lubricant that is secreted by root cap cells.

Mycorrhizal fungi—Soil fungi that associate with plant roots to increase the absorption area in return for sugars.

Myosin—A molecular motor that moves along microfilaments.

Netted venation—An arrangement of vascular bundles in which they regularly branch and intersect like a net.

Nitrogenous base—Nitrogen-containing component of DNA and RNA.

Node—Region of the stem where leaves or branches form.

Nuclear envelope—Porous, double membrane that surrounds the nucleus.

Nucleolus—A region of the nucleus where ribosomes are transcribed.

Nucleus—An organelle of eukaryotic cells that contains DNA.

Opposite—Leaf arrangement in which there are two leaves per node.

Organ—A structure that is composed of multiple tissues (e.g., root, stem, or leaf).

Organelle—A membrane-bound component of the cell, such as the endoplasmic reticulum, Golgi bodies, plastids, mitochondria, nucleus, or vacuole.

Osmosis—Diffusion of water across a semipermeable membrane.

Outer bark—The dead tissues that lie outside of the youngest cork cambium in plants that have undergone secondary growth.

Palisade parenchyma—Vertically oriented, columnar mesophyll cells of leaves that contain many chloroplasts.

Palmately compound—Describes a leaf whose leaflets originate from a common point.

Parallel venation—Arrangement of vascular bundles such that the major veins run parallel to each other along the length of a leaf.

Parenchyma—Unspecialized cells with thin cell walls or a ground-tissue type of many such cells.

Glossary

Passage cell—An endodermal cell that has only a Casparian strip for a waterproof barrier when others become totally suberized or waterproofed; the chief water-conducting cell of an older epidermis.

Pectin—Material that gels the cell wall and cements adjacent cells together.

Perennial—A plant that lives for multiple years.

Pericycle—The outermost cylinder of vascular tissue in the root, surrounded by the endodermis.

Periderm—Protective tissue that replaces the epidermis in stems and roots that have undergone secondary growth.

Petiole—Leaf stalk that joins the blade to the stem.

Phelloderm—Living parenchymatous cells that are produced by the cork cambium; the inner part of the periderm.

Phloem—Conductive tissue that transports sugars.

Phloem sap—Dissolved sugars and other organic molecules that flow through sieve tubes.

Photosynthesis—A process by which the energy of sunlight is used to convert carbon dioxide into sugar.

Phragmoplast—An array of microtubules that forms between the maturing daughter nuclei during the final stage of cell division.

Phragmosome—A sheet of cytoplasm that bisects the cell and suspends the nucleus in its center.

Phyllotaxy—Arrangement of leaves along the stem.

Pinnately compound—Describes a leaf whose leaflets are arranged along a central axis (rachis).

Pith—A central region of parenchymatous cells in some stems and roots.

Plasma membrane—Outer layer of the protoplast between the cell wall and the cytosol; made of lipids and proteins.

Plasmodesma—A membrane-lined channel that connects adjacent cells.

Plastid—An organelle specific to plants and algae. Plastids are surrounded by two lipid bilayers and include chloroplasts, chromoplasts, and leucoplasts.

Polar microtubule—An extension of the mitotic spindle that does not attach to a kinetochore, but rather pushes the two asters apart.

Polyarch—Describes a root with more than four protoxylem poles.

Polymerize—Many parts coming together, as in microtubule assembly by tubulin.

Polypeptide—A chain of amino acids. One or more polypeptides make a protein.

Polysaccharide—A long chain of many sugars, linked together.

Pore size—The width of an opening, such as that of a stoma or plasmodesma.

Preprophase band—A ring of microtubules that forms during interphase and facilitates cell division.

Pressure-flow hypothesis—A model that explains phloem sap movement through sieve tubes by way of a turgor pressure gradient.

Primary cell wall—Outermost covering of the cell that is produced following division, rich in cellulose and pectins.

Primary meristem—One of three tissue precursors created by the apical meristem. Includes procambium, ground meristem, and protoderm.

Primary plant body—The plant, prior to secondary growth.

Primary plasmodesma—Plasmodesma formed during cell division.

Procambium—Primary meristem that produces vascular tissues.

Prokaryote—A single-celled organism without a nucleus or membranous organelles; bacteria and archaea are prokaryotes.

Prophase—The first stage of mitosis, in which DNA condenses into chromosomes and the nucleus breaks down.

Protein—A large, complex molecule made of many amino acids.

Protoderm—Primary meristem that produces dermal tissues.

Protoplast—All of the plant cell excluding its cell wall.

Protoxylem—Xylem that differentiates in a region that is elongating.

Protoxylem pole—Primary water-conducting cells that form a ridge near the pericycle of the root.

Glossary

Rachis—Main axis of a compound leaf.

Radicle—The root of an embryo.

Ray—A radial file of parenchyma cells in organs that have undergone secondary growth.

Ray initial—Meristematic cell of the vascular cambium that divides horizontally to produce a radial file of parenchyma cells (ray).

Region of cell division—Youngest part of the root in which cells are actively dividing.

Respiration—Chemical process that converts sugar into energy (ATP).

Rhizome—An underground stem that has been modified for storage, as in ginger.

Ribosome—A molecule that facilitates the synthesis of amino acids into polypeptides.

RNA (ribonucleic acid)—A single-stranded molecule involved in transcription of a gene and translation into a polypeptide.

Root apical meristem—A self-perpetuating region of undifferentiated cells at the tip of the belowground portion of the plant, from which new cells arise.

Root cap—Cells at the root tip that protect the apical meristem.

Root cortex—A large region of ground tissue that lies beneath the epidermis.

Root hair—A tubular projection of a root epidermal cell that increases the area of contact with the soil.

Rough ER—Endoplasmic reticulum that is coated with ribosomes.

Sapwood—Younger, water-conducting xylem near the outside of tree trunks.

Sclereid—Short sclerenchyma cells, variable in shape.

Sclerenchyma—Ground-tissue type composed of tough cells with thick secondary walls.

Secondary cell wall—Innermost covering of the cell, usually rich in a strong material such as lignin.

Secondary growth—Lateral thickening of stems or roots involving production of new vascular and dermal tissues by cambia.

Secondary phloem—Sugar-conducting tissue produced by the vascular cambium.

Secondary plasmodesma—Plasmodesma created after cell division.

Secondary xylem—Water-conducting tissue produced by the vascular cambium.

Secretion—A process by which material is delivered to the outside of a cell.

Seed—A dormant, young plant surrounded by nourishing tissues and a protective coat.

Semi-permeable—Membranes that permit free passage of some molecules, like water, but block the passage of others.

Sessile—A leaf with no petiole.

Sheath—A leaf base that wraps around the stem, as in corn leaves.

Shoot apical meristem—A self-perpetuating region of undifferentiated cells at the tip of the aboveground portion of the plant, from which new cells arise.

Sieve plate—Perforated end of a sieve tube element through which phloem sap must pass in order to move through the sieve tube.

Sieve tube—A long, narrow column formed by stacked phloem cells.

Sieve tube element—Sugar-conducting cell type in phloem tissue, alive at maturity.

Simple—A leaf whose blade is not divided into leaflets.

Sink—Site of sugar usage, as in rapidly growing regions or storage roots.

Sister chromatids—Two identical DNA molecules that are produced by DNA duplication and, together with a centromere, form a chromosome.

Smooth ER—Endoplasmic reticulum that is not coated with ribosomes.

Source—Site of sugar production in leaves.

Specialization—Adaptation to a particular function or environment.

Glossary

Spindle fibers—Bundles of microtubules within the mitotic spindle.

S Phase—Period of interphase in which DNA replicates itself.

Spine—Modified leaf or stipule that is hard, nonphotosynthetic, and pointed.

Spongy parenchyma—Photosynthetic mesophyll cells in leaves with many intercellular airspaces surrounding them.

Spore—The product of meiosis in plants.

Spring wood—Secondary xylem that is produced in the spring.

Starch—A branched molecule of many sugars linked together.

Stele—The vascular cylinder in the center of roots and some stems.

Stipule—One of a pair of leaf-like appendages located at the petiole-stem junction of some plants.

Stolon—A horizontally spreading stem that grows along the ground and produces new plants.

Stoma—An epidermal pore found on the surface of leaves and stems, as well as its surrounding guard cells, through which gases are exchanged.

Stop codon—Three consecutive nitrogenous bases on mRNA that terminate polypeptide synthesis.

Stroma—The fluid within the inner membrane of plastids.

Suberin—A fatty, waterproof substance that coats cork and endodermal cells.

Succulent—Juicy and fleshy.

Summer wood—Secondary xylem that is produced in the summer.

Symplast—The shared cytoplasm of multiple cells.

Symplastic domain—The collection of cells that are connected by plasmodesmata.

Symplastic movement—The passage from one cell to another via plasmodesmata.

Taproot—The main root axis of some plants, off of which smaller roots branch.

Taproot system—The central main root axis plus all of its subsidiary roots.

Telophase—The fourth and final stage of mitosis, in which daughter nuclei form around the separated chromosomes.

Tendril—Modified organ that coils around existing structures, which helps the plant climb.

Tetrarch—A root with four protoxylem poles.

Thorn—A modified stem, often woody, with a sharp point.

Thylakoid—The membrane system within the inner membrane of plastids. In chloroplasts, the thylakoid contains the pigments necessary for light capture during photosynthesis.

Thymine—A nitrogenous base in DNA.

Tissue—A collection of cells with similar structure or function.

Tissue system—An aggregation of tissues that share function, continuity, and meristematic precursor cells. Three tissue systems exist in plants: dermal, ground, and vascular.

TMV (tobacco mosaic virus)—Plant pathogen that moves from cell to cell via plasmodesmata.

Tonoplast—A single lipid bilayer that surrounds the vacuole.

Tracheary element—A water-conducting cell, including tracheids and vessel elements.

Tracheid—Long, water-conducting xylem cell that is found in both gymnosperms and angiosperms.

Transcription—The process by which a gene's information is stored in a strand of RNA.

Transfer RNA (tRNA)—A folded RNA molecule that binds to a specific mRNA codon and adds an amino acid to a growing polypeptide.

Translation—The process by which an mRNA sequence is decoded into the amino acid sequence of the resulting polypeptide.

Transpiration—The process of water loss, including both the evaporation of liquid water into a gas and diffusion of gaseous water out of the leaf.

Glossary

Triarch—A root with three protoxylem poles.

Trichome—An epidermal outgrowth of the shoot, such as a leaf hair.

Tuber—An underground stem that has been modified for storage, as in potatoes.

Tubulin—The protein subunits that make up microtubules.

Turgor—Positive pressure exerted on the cell wall by the protoplast; confers rigidity to nonwoody plants.

Undifferentiated—Without special physical or biochemical features.

Uracil—A nitrogenous base in RNA.

Vacuole—Fluid-filled organelle within the cell, often accounting for most of a cell's volume.

Vascular cambium—A lateral meristem that produces secondary xylem and phloem.

Vascular tissue system—All of the conductive tissues and the tissues that produce them, such as xylem, phloem, and vascular cambia.

Vein—A bundle of vascular tissue in a leaf.

Venation—Pattern of vein arrangement in leaves.

Vessel—A column of conductive xylem cells that form a continuous tube.

Vessel elements—Water-conducting xylem cells in angiosperms that die at maturity.

Vine—A plant that must climb up another plant or structure for support.

Virus—A microscopic entity that requires a host cell to duplicate itself.

Whorled—A leaf arrangement in which there are three or more leaves per node.

Wilting—A process in which nonwoody plants become limp due to lack of turgor (often due to lack of water).

Xylem—Water-conducting vascular tissue.

Zygote—The product of two gametes that have fused together.

Apples and Wax. Accessed on http://www.usapple.org/consumers/wax.cfm.

Bailey, J., ed. *The Penguin Dictionary of Plant Sciences*. New York: Penguin Putnam Inc., 1999.

Bel, A., J.E. van, and J. P. van Kesteren Wilhelmus, eds. *Plasmodesmata: Structure, Function, Role in Cell Communication*. New York: Springer, 1999.

Brown, D. *Aroids: Plants of the Arum Family*. 2nd ed. Portland: Timber Press, 2000.

Campbell, N.A., J.B. Reece, and L.G. Mitchell. *Biology*. 5th ed. Menlo Park, Calif.: Benjamin/Cummings, 1999.

Coile, N.C. "*Urtica chamaedryoides* Pursh: A Stinging Nettle, or Fireweed and Some Related Species." *Botany Circular* 34 (September/October 1999), 1–6, http://www.doacs.state.fl.us/pi/enpp/botany/botcirc/Botcirc34.pdf.

Deepest Root. Accessed on http://www.guinnessworldrecords.com.

Dickison, W.C. *Integrative Plant Anatomy*. San Diego: Academic Press, 2000.

Dittmer, H.J. "A Quantitative Study of the Roots and Root Hairs of a Winter Rye Plant (*Secale Cereale*)." *American Journal of Botany* 24, no. 7 (1937): 417–20.

Dyall, S.D., M.T. Brown, and P.J. Johnson. "Ancient Invasions: From Endosymbionts to Organelles." *Science* 304 (2004): 253–57.

Gunning, B. E. S., and M.W. Steer. *Ultrastructure and the Biology of Plant Cells*. London: Edward Arnold, 1975.

Harris, J.G., and M.W. Harris. *Plant Identification and Terminology: An Illustrated Glossary*. 2nd ed. Spring Lake, Utah: Spring Lake Publishing, 2001.

International Carnivorous Plant Society (ICPS). Accessed on http://www.carnivorousplants.org.

Pan, J.W. , D. Ye, L.L. Wang, et al. "Root Border Cell Development is a Temperature-Insensitive and Al-Sensitive Process in Barley." *Plant Cell Physiology* 45, no. 6 (2004): 751–60.

Kaiser, D. "Building a Multicellular Organism," *Annual Review of Genetics* 35 (2001): 103–23.

Bibliography

Kirk, J. T. O., and R. A. E. Tilney-Bassett. *The Plastids: Their Chemistry, Structure, Growth and Inheritance.* 2nd ed. New York: Elsevier/North Holland Biomedical Press, 1978.

Lucas, W. J., and J.Y. Lee. "Plasmodesmata as a Supracellular Control Network in Plants." *Nature Reviews, Molecular Cell Biology* 5 (2004): 712–26.

Maddison, D. R., and K. -S. Schulz, ed. "Life on Earth." *The Tree of Life Web Project,* http://tolweb.org.

Maple Facts. Accessed on http://www.vermontmaple.org.

Maple History. Accessed on http://www.massmaple.org/history.html.

McIntosh, J. R., E. L. Grishchuk, and R.R. West. "Chromosome-Microtubule Interactions During Mitosis." *Annual Review of Cell and Developmental Biology* 18 (2002): 193–219.

Nelson, D. L., and M. M. Cox. *Lehninger Principles of Biochemistry.* 3rd ed. New York: W. H. Freeman & Company, 2000.

Northeast Forest Experiment Station. *Sugar Maple Research: Sap Production, Processing, and Marketing of Maple Syrup.* Broomall, Pa. U.S. Department of Agriculture, Forest Service, Northeastern Forest Experiment Station, 1982.

Porsild, A. E., C. R. Harington, and G. A. Mulligan. "*Lupinus arcticus* Wats. Grown from Seeds of Pleistocene Age." *Science* 158 (1967): 113–14.

Raven, P. H., R. F. Evert, and S. E. Eichhorn. *Biology of Plants.* 6th ed. New York: W. H. Freeman and Company, 1999.

Rickson, F. R. "Ultrastructural Differentiation of the Mullerian Body Glycogen Plastid of *Cecropia peltata* L." *American Journal of Botany* 63, no. 9 (1976): 1272–79.

Robinsin, D.G., and J. C. Rogers. *Vacuolar Compartments.* Boca Raton, Fla.: CRC Press, 2000.

Rudman, W. B. "Solar-powered Sea Slugs." *The Sea Slug Forum,* http://www.seaslugforum.net/factsheet.cfm?base=solarpow.

Rumpho, M. E., E. J. Summer, and J. R. Manhart. "Solar-Powered Sea Slugs. Mollusc/Algal Chloroplast Symbiosis." *Plant Physiology* 1230 (2000): 29–38.

Sack, F. D. "Plastids and Gravitropic Sensing." *Planta* 203 (1997): S63–S68.

Shorthouse, J. D., and O. Rohfritsch, eds. *Biology of Insect-Induced Galls.* New York: Oxford University Press, 1992.

Smith, L. G. "Plant Cell Division: Building Walls in the Right Places." *Nature Reviews, Molecular Cell Biology* 2 (2001): 33–39.

Sugaring Story, The. Accessed on www.vermontmaple.org.

The Arabidopsis Information Resource (TAIR). "About *Arabidopsis thaliana*." http://arabidopsis.org.

Thurston, E. L. "Morphology, Fine Structure, and Ontogeny of the Stinging Emergence of *Urtica dioica*," *American Journal of Botany* 61, no. 8 (1974): 809–17.

U.S. Department of the Treasury. "Frequently Asked Questions: Currency," http://www.treas.gov/education/faq/currency/production.shtml.

Vothknect, U. C., and P. Westhoff. "Biogenesis and Origin of Thylakoid Membranes." *Biochimica et Biophysica Acta* 1541 (2001): 91–101.

Walnut Shell Products. Accessed on www.compomat.com/walnut-2.shtml.

Williams, M. A. J., ed. *Plant Galls: Organisms, Interactions, Populations.* New York: Oxford University Press Inc., 1994.

Further Reading

Attenborough, D. *The Private Life of Plants*. Princeton, NJ: Princeton University Press, 1995.

Bailey, J., ed. *The Penguin Dictionary of Plant Sciences*. New York: Penguin Putnam Inc., 1999.

Bel, A., J.E. van, and J. P. van Kesteren Wilhelmus, eds. *Plasmodesmata: Structure, Function, Role in Cell Communication*. New York: Springer, 1999.

Bewley, J. D., M. Black. *Seeds: Physiology of Development and Germination*. New York: Plenum Press, 1994.

Blackmore, S., and E. Tootill, eds. *The Facts on File Dictionary of Botany*. New York: Facts on File, 1984.

Dickison, W.C. *Integrative Plant Anatomy*. San Diego: Academic Press, 2000.

Durrell, G. *A Practical Guide for the Amateur Naturalist*. London: Alfred A. Knopf, 1982.

Erickson, J. *A History of Life on Earth: Understanding Our Planet's Past*. New York: Facts on File, 1995.

Galston, A.W. *Life Processes of Plants*. New York: Scientific American Library, 1994.

Harris, J.G., and M.W. Harris. *Plant Identification and Terminology: An Illustrated Glossary*. 2d ed. Spring Lake, Utah: Spring Lake Publishing, 2001.

Hopkins, W. G. and N. P. A. Hüner. *Introduction to Plant Physiology*. 3rd ed. New York: John Wiley & Sons, 2004.

Raven, P. H., R. F. Evert, and S. E. Eichhorn. *Biology of Plants*. 6th ed. New York: W. H. Freeman and Company, 1999.

Robinsin, D.G., and J. C. Rogers. *Vacuolar Compartments*. Boca Raton, Fla.: CRC Press, 2000.

Shorthouse, J. D., and O. Rohfritsch, eds. *Biology of Insect-Induced Galls*. New York: Oxford University Press, 1992.

Williams, M. A. J., ed. *Plant Galls: Organisms, Interactions, Populations*. New York: Oxford University Press Inc., 1994.

Index

Endoplasmic reticulum (ER), 19
    during cell division, 43, 49, 66
    cisternae, 21
    lumen, 20–22
    and the plasmodesmata, 36–38
    rough, 21–23
    smooth, 21–22, 66
Endosymbiosis, 39
Epicotyl, 72
Epiphytes, 5–6
ER. *see* Endoplasmic reticulum
Eukaryotes
    cytoskeleton, 5
    energy requirements, 21
    features of, 11, 14, 17, 25, 28–39
    nucleus, 5, 17–19, 22, 28

Fungi, 28, 50

Galls, 50
Gene, 38
    bacteria-like, 25
    transcription, 18–19
    translation, 18–20
    variability, 42, 49, 51–53
Golgi body
    during cell division, 43, 49, 65
    cisternae, 21–22
    polysaccharide production, 21
Ground tissue system, 56, 67
    collenchyma, 57–60, 73, 105
    in leaves, 100, 104–106
    parenchyma, 57–59, 63, 65–66,
        73–74, 91, 104, 106
    in roots, 91, 100
    sclerenchyma, 57–59, 61, 73,
        105
    in stems, 71, 73, 100
Gymnosperms, 76, 76
    examples of, 7, 62, 74, 86

Herbaceous plants, 74, 76
Herbivores, 30, 36, 109

Hooke, Robert, 7–8
Hydrophytes, 5

Interphase, 47
    G_1 phase, 42–43
    G_2 phase, 42–44
    S phase, 42–43

Leaves, 11, 50, 67
    compound, 100
    diversity, 107–109
    functions, 98–101, 103, 105, 107,
        109
    growth, 100
    light-capturing, 70, 73, 98–99, 103
    morphology, 99–100
    simple, 100
    structures, 60–61, 71–72, 84,
        100–107, 109
Leucoplasts
    amyloplasts, 35, 37, 91
    functions, 35–37
    and glycogen, 36
    and starch, 35
Lipids, 21, 33
    bilayer, 14–15, 17, 20, 23, 30, 32
    hydrophilic, 14–15
    hydrophobic, 14–15
Lysosomes, 31

Meiosis I, 49
    anaphase I, 52–53
    metaphase I, 51–53
    prophase I, 51–53
    spores, 50–51, 53
    telophase I, 52–53
Meiosis II, 52–53
Mitochondria, 8, 32
    during cell division, 43, 65
    cristae, 23, 25
    functions, 21–25, 38–39
    matrix, 25
    respiration, 21, 23–24, 39

Index

Roots, 11, 50, 67
    absorption, 30, 56–57, 64–65, 87–88, 90–91, 93, 98–99
    anchorage and storage, 56, 87, 94
    apical meristem, 89
    cap, 89
    fibrous root system, 84
    functions, 35–36, 84–89
    mucigel, 89
    primary growth, 84, 86–90
    secondary growth, 84, 90, 94–95, 100
    structure, 70–71, 84–85, 89–94, 100–101
    taproot system, 84, 86–87

Scale, 10
Secretion, 16
Seed plants, 5–6, 30
    classes of, 7
    germination, 6, 84–85
    tissues of, 11, 74
Specialization, 56
Stems, 11, 50, 67
    functions, 70, 94, 98
    morphological diversity of, 79–81
    primary growth, 70, 73, 75, 87
    secondary growth, 74–78, 94, 100
    shoot structures, 57, 71–72, 74–75, 79, 84–85, 87, 90, 100
    tissue organization, 71, 73–75

Thermogenesis, 24
Tissues, 31, 90
    defined, 11, 56
    dermal system, 56–57, 67, 71, 73–74, 78–79, 88, 90–91, 93, 95, 100–105

ground system, 56–61, 67, 71, 73–74, 91, 100, 104–106
    organization of, 10–11
    vascular system, 56, 61–67, 71, 73–78, 88, 90, 92–95, 98, 100, 106–107
TMV. *See* Tobacco mosaic virus
Tobacco mosaic virus (TMV), 39
Transcription, 18–19
Translation, 18–20
Transpiration, 99
Trichomes, 101–102, 104
Turgor, 30

Vacuole, 28
    during cell division, 43, 65
    cell sap, 30–31
    defense compounds in, 31
    functions, 31
    pigments in, 31
    tonoplast, 30
    toxic chemicals in, 31
Vascular tissue system, 56, 61
    in leaves, 100, 106–107
    parenchyma, 63, 65–66, 73–74, 76, 94
    phloem, 62–63, 65–67, 74–75, 77–78, 93–95, 106–107
    procambium, 62, 92
    in roots, 88, 90, 92–95, 100
    secondary growth, 76–78
    in stems, 71, 73–78, 100
    xylem, 62–65, 74–75, 77–78, 88, 93–95, 98, 106–107
Viruses, 7, 39, 50

Wilting, 30

page:

6: Carlyn Iverson/
Photo Researchers, Inc

8: Russell Kightley/
Photo Researchers, Inc

15: National Institutes of Health/
Photo Researchers, Inc

22: Francis Leroy, Biocosmos/
Photo Researchers, Inc

23: Keith R. Porter/
Photo Researchers, Inc

29: Photo Researchers, Inc.

33: Dr Jeremy Burgess/
Photo Researchers, Inc

35: Richard J. Green/
Photo Researchers, Inc

37: Dr. Jeremy Burgess/
Photo Researchers, Inc

45: M. I. Walker/Photo Researchers, Inc

48: Joshua T. Williams

52: Joshua T. Williams

59: Andrew Syred/
Photo Researchers, Inc

60: Eye of Science/
Photo Researchers, Inc

65: SPL/Photo Researchers, Inc

72: Scherer Illustration

75: James E. Bell/
Photo Researchers, Inc

78: Sidney Moulds/
Photo Researchers, Inc

80: Sheila Terry/
Photo Researchers, Inc

85: Dr. Jeremy Burgess/
Photo Researchers, Inc

86: Lynwood M. Chace/
Photo Researchers, Inc

92: Andrew Syred/
Photo Researchers, Inc

93: Francis Leroy, Biocosmos/
Photo Researchers, Inc

105: Dr Jeremy Burgess/
Photo Researchers, Inc

106: Francis Leroy, Biocosmos/
Photo Researchers, Inc

108: F. Stuart Westmorland/Photo
Researchers, Inc (top)

108: Simon Fraser/Photo Researchers,
Inc (bottom)

Cover: Corel/Royalty free photograph

About the Author

Nicholas Stephens is studying at the University of Wisconsin-Madison for his doctoral degree from the Department of Botany. Nicholas is a research assistant for Dr. Edgar Spalding and studies plant proteins that are similar to neurotransmitter receptors of animal brains. He holds a bachelor's degree in both biology and botany from the University of Washington in Seattle, Washington, where he participated in studies ranging from rhododendron genetics to electrical signaling in sunflowers. He has received several academic awards and scholarships and participates in outreach programs for elementary students. Nicholas presently resides in Madison, Wisconsin, with his beloved Hillary.